ROUTLEDGE LIBRARY EDITIONS: COMPARATIVE EDUCATION

Volume 1

THE RUSSIAN INFLUENCE ON ENGLISH EDUCATION

THE RUSSIAN INFLUENCE ON ENGLISH EDUCATION

W. H. G. ARMYTAGE

LONDON AND NEW YORK

First published in 1969 by Routledge & Kegan Paul Ltd

This edition first published in 2018
by Routledge
2 Park Square, Milton Park, Abingdon, Oxon OX14 4RN

and by Routledge
711 Third Avenue, New York, NY 10017

Routledge is an imprint of the Taylor & Francis Group, an informa business

© 1969 W. H. G. Armytage

All rights reserved. No part of this book may be reprinted or reproduced or utilised in any form or by any electronic, mechanical, or other means, now known or hereafter invented, including photocopying and recording, or in any information storage or retrieval system, without permission in writing from the publishers.

Trademark notice: Product or corporate names may be trademarks or registered trademarks, and are used only for identification and explanation without intent to infringe.

British Library Cataloguing in Publication Data
A catalogue record for this book is available from the British Library

ISBN: 978-1-138-54113-9 (Set)
ISBN: 978-1-351-00358-2 (Set) (ebk)
ISBN: 978-1-138-54399-7 (Volume 1) (hbk)
ISBN: 978-1-351-00526-5 (Volume 1) (ebk)

Publisher's Note
The publisher has gone to great lengths to ensure the quality of this reprint but points out that some imperfections in the original copies may be apparent.

Disclaimer
The publisher has made every effort to trace copyright holders and would welcome correspondence from those they have been unable to trace.

The Russian Influence on English Education

by W. H. G. Armytage

LONDON
ROUTLEDGE & KEGAN PAUL
NEW YORK: HUMANITIES PRESS

First published 1969
by Routledge & Kegan Paul Ltd
Broadway House, 68–74 Carter Lane
London E.C.4
Printed in Great Britain
by Willmer Brothers Limited
Birkenhead, Cheshire
© W. H. G. Armytage 1969
No part of this book may be reproduced
in any form without permission from
the publisher, except for the quotation
of brief passages in criticism
SBN 7100 6492 6

THE STUDENTS LIBRARY OF EDUCATION has been designed to meet the needs of students of Education at Colleges of Education and at University Institutes and Departments. It will also be valuable for practising teachers and educationists. The series takes full account of the latest developments in teacher-training and of new methods and approaches in education. Separate volumes will provide authoritative and up-to-date accounts of the topics within the major fields of sociology, philosophy and history of education, educational psychology, and method. Care has been taken that specialist topics are treated lucidly and usefully for the non-specialist reader. Altogether, the Students' Library of Education will provide a comprehensive introduction and guide to anyone concerned with the study of education, and with educational theory and practice.

J. W. TIBBLE

It will come as a surprise to many to know that British merchants first penetrated to Moscow as early as the 16th century. From that time until today developments in Russia have influenced Britain in innumerable ways—sometimes unexpectedly. In this volume, Professor Armytage traces this influence, showing how Tolstoy, Kropotkin, and others better known for their activities in fields other than education have, in fact, held opinions or carried out activities which have had their effect on education in this country. Recently, of course, this influence has been more direct, particularly in stimulating the more rapid development of higher technological education than might otherwise have been the case. If Tolstoy visited English schools in the company of Matthew Arnold, his famous school at Yasnaya Polyana had its imitators also in this country. This is only one example of the mutual influence of the two countries which, as Professor Armytage shows, has a longer history than is generally known. With this volume, in the history series of the Students' Library, Professor Armytage completes his group of volumes on foreign influences on British education.

B.S.

Contents

	Preface	page xi
1	**Muscovy and the merchant marine**	
	Naval storehouse	1
	Feedback	2
	Setback	3
	The first 'county schools'	5
	Hull Trinity House School	7
	Magnet for talent	8
2	**Spiritual affairs and national instruction**	
	John Brown's enthusiasm for state church control	10
	Benthamite laboratory	12
	Partners in propaganda	14
	The Russian Ministry cited	16
	From the St Petersburg marshes to Hampshire	18
3	**Polish exiles**	
	The first wave: 1830	20
	The second wave: 1851	22
	The third wave: 1863	23

CONTENTS

4 The aftermath of the Crimean War: 1854-1867
Essential expertise 24
Competence vs cousinhood 26
The war and popular education 27
The rise of B.S.A. 29
The military and Russia 29

5 Nihilism and science
Bazarov: the embodiment of nihilism 31
G. H. Lewes and his contributors 32
Wallace and the Russian challenge 33
Early warnings of Russia's technical intelligentsia 35
The premonitions of Seeley and others 37
The War Office again 38
Darlington's report: 1909 39
Russian science in England 41
Russian exiles: Kropotkin and his friends 42
The fifth wave: the Jews 45

6 Ecumenical efforts
Epiklesis vs economics 48
Holy Russia 49
The Eastern Church Association 51
New forms of religious experience 53

7 Tolstoy and his English exegetes
Yasnaya Polyana 54
Tolstoy and Matthew Arnold 55
The English Tolstovitsi (i) the colonies 56
The English Tolstovitsi (ii) the cells 58
D. H. Lawrence and his friends 60
The Garnett circle 62

8 The Red bogey: 1919-1930
The polarization of feeling towards the Soviets 64

CONTENTS

	Three travellers' reports	65
	The Trade Union delegation of 1920	67
	The Zinoviev letter	68
	The death of the Liberal Party	69
	The Trade Union delegation of 1924	70
	The revival of the 'religious question' in English education	71
9	Mediators and interpreters	
	Berdyaev and the Y.M.C.A.	74
	P.E.P.	76
	H. G. Wells	77
	The young scientists	78
	S.C.R. and A.Sc.W.	80
	The C.P.G.B.	81
	The polytechnic principle	84
	Sympathy from 'old India hands'	85
10	Whiffs of realism: 1929-1941	
	Businessmen and teachers	87
	Films	88
	Bertrand Russell	89
	Technology and society	90
	Russian progress (i) technical training	91
	Russian progress (ii) a National Health Policy	92
	Lord Simon's first warning, 1937	93
	The Left Book Club	95
	The Webbs' report	96
11	The Second World War and after: 1941-1957	
	Communism and managerialism	99
	Pressure for the comprehensive school	100
	The debate about the crisis in universities	101
	Lord Simon's second warning, 1956	103
	Russia in Europe	105

CONTENTS

12 The post-sputnik era: 1957-1969
- The galvanizing of the U.S.A. — 108
- Lord Simon's third warning, 1960 — 109
- Sir Leon Bagrit and day boarding schools — 111
- The spirit of Makarenko — 113
- The influence of Strumilin — 115
- The 1958 and 1964 reforms — 117
- Anglo-Russian co-operation — 118

13 Conclusion
- The dead-end of all discussion — 120
- The real iron curtain — 121
- The re-orientation of humanistic studies in English universities — 122
- The challenge of motivation — 123
- Belief in educability — 125

Bibliography — 129

Preface

Free, compulsory, secular education, in a society based on switch-controlled power, characterized the imaginary world of the future projected by Thaddeus Bulgarin, one of Russia's earliest Utopians. His writings led the English *Foreign Quarterly Review* to describe him in 1831 as paving 'the way to an acquaintance with the literature of a country which has hitherto led out nothing sufficiently promising to entice us to encounter the labour of acquiring its language' (Vol. 18, p. 139). Certainly Bulgarin's world of the future, with its prefabricated buildings, dehydrated food, self-propelled cars, sea farms, lie-detectors and emotion-analysing machines, was a very advanced one even by early nineteenth-century standards (Vaslef, 1968, p. 37). Subsequently others of his fellow countrymen explored the implications of such a technological Utopia: Chernyshevsky (whose writings converted Lenin to communism), Dostoievsky (of whom Virginia Woolf said that 'out of Shakespeare there is no more exciting reading') (Woolf, 1932, p. 226) and Zamyatin (who influenced George Orwell's *1984*).

By the time of Zamyatin, Bulgarin's Utopian dream looked like a dystopian nightmare; the British image of

Russia oscillated between these two poles, tending to remain longer at the second. Nor had the *Foreign Quarterly Review's* hope that Bulgarin's work would pave the way to a better understanding of the Russian language been adequately fulfilled, so that many Englishmen have tended to draw inferences from, rather than be influenced by, Russian practice over the years. Indeed this present book might well have been entitled *Inferences from Russia in English Educational History*. But since inferences involve the acceptance of evidence (or, more important still, of premises), 'influence', with its overtones of insensibility and invisibility, seems a more relevant concept around which to focus the story told in the following pages.

Today the significance of Russian education is more in the heavens above than in any conceptual heaven ahead. Yet there are still some who take the view first expressed by Werner Keller in his *Ost Minus West=Null* (1960)—a book translated in the following year by Constantine Fitzgibbon under the title *Are the Russians Ten Feet Tall?*—that 'If the Russians had never existed at all it would have made not an iota of difference to what the West has to offer all humanity'. I do not hold this view. Experience in looking at England's relations to Russia from a non-involved observation point encourages me to hope that students might find some value in the leads indicated in the following pages—cursory, alas, because of the nature of the series. To help them enlarge upon, or otherwise exploit, these leads in projects and essays, a bibliography, keyed to the text, is provided. For those anxious to monitor recent changes in Russian education, the relevant sections in *Soviet Studies* have, since 1949, offered invaluable help.

Russia is a country about which it is very hard to avoid exaggeration you have to... avoid all neutral tints if you wish to produce anything like an accurate portraiture of this extraordinary land.

EDWARD DICEY, *A Month in Russia*,
London: Macmillan, 1867, p. 104

We have each a good deal to learn from the Russians, if we are not too proud. Incidentally, the Russians have a good deal to learn from us too. Isn't it time we began? The danger is, we have been brought up to think as though we had all the time in the world. We have very little time. So little that I dare not guess at it.

C. P. SNOW, *The Two Cultures: and a Second Look*,
Cambridge University Press, 1964, pp. 50-1

1
Muscovy and the merchant marine

Naval storehouse·

All studies and letters of humanitie they utterly refuse: concerning the Latine, Greeke, and Hebrew tongues, they are altogether ignorant in them. (Hakluyt, 1903, p. 266).

So, in 1553, Richard Chancellor reported on the Russians to his employers, the Muscovy Company—the first joint-stock corporation to be chartered by the British government for the discovery of 'lands, territories etc. unknown'. By opening a channel, albeit exiguous, to Muscovy, he made it possible for a commercial treaty to be signed, allowing British ships to sail down the Volga. A Russian ambassador came to England and contacts were established between the two countries. True, these were not the first. As we have often been told, the present Queen Elizabeth II is descended in the thirty-first generation from Volodymyr Monomakh, Prince of the Ukraine, who married Gytha, the daughter of Harold who was killed at Hastings.

The first Muscovy Merchants were given what became known as the English House in Varvanka Street, now No 12 Razin Street. From here correspondence shuttled to

THE RUSSIAN INFLUENCE ON ENGLISH EDUCATION

England inviting architects, doctors, apothecaries and assayers. Parts of the house survived the fire of 29 January 1612, and today (1968) it is under process of restoration as a national monument.

As England's naval chandlery, Russia supplied timber, flax, fur, hemp, potash, wax and iron—all desperately needed. So important was the rope industry to England that English artisans went over to instruct Russians in its manufacture. In spite of Russia's vast area and terrible winters, the Muscovy Company obtained outlets for the English cloth trade and nascent medicament industry, and sent these goods in exchange for naval goods. The nature of the goods sent to Russia roused suspicions amongst Russia's neighbours. The King of Poland spoke for them when he wrote:

> The Moscovite, enemy to all liberty under the heavens, dayly to grow mightier by the increase of such (English) things as be brought to the Narve, while not only wares but also weapons heretofore unknowen to him, and artificers and arts be brought unto him. by meane whereof he maketh himselfe strong to vanquish all others... We Seemed hitherto to vanquish him onely in this, that he was rude of arts, and ignorant of policies. If so be that this navigation to the Narve continue, what shall be unknown to him? (Simmons, 1935, p. 22).

Feedback

Other pointers to the relationships that were to exist between Russia and England can be seen at this time. The first was the portrait of Russian autocracy in Giles Fletcher's *Of the Russe Commonwealth* (1591)—a contrast to the more flexible English method of government. So pointed was this book that it was suppressed in England lest it hurt trade. The second pointer was the disappearance of four Russian students who were sent to England in 1601. One of them was subsequently discovered to have become an Anglican clergyman (Simmons, 1935, p. 32). Third, there began an enthusiastic, but poorly maintained study of the Russian language (Leeming, 1968, pp. 1-30), 'the most copious and elegant language in the world' according to Jeremy Horsey (Hakluyt Society, 1856, p. 156). Fourth, there began a slow but perceptible feedback into the educational system. The Muscovy Company maintained a lecturer in cosmography to instruct sailors, retailing no doubt the careful observations made by the voyagers of 1553 and afterwards. They also financed Richard Eden's translation of Cortes' *Art of Navigation*, published in 1561. Russian words crept into English (Leeming, 1968, pp. 1-30), and Mark Ridley, a doctor, compiled a manuscript Dictionary—now in the Bodleian. T. S. Willan, however, thinks that 'the intangible gains cannot have been very great to either country' (Willan, 1956, p. 284).

As England's overseas possessions grew in the West, some thought that we should pull out of the East. Thus, a writer argued in 1608 that 'since Muscovia and Polonia doe yearly receive manie thousands for pitch, tarre, scrap ashes, resin, flax cordage, sturgeon, masts, yardes, waynscot, furres, glasse, and such like', Virginia might well supply them (Albion, 1926, pp. 230-1). Significantly the first cargo of masts did come from Virginia in 1609. But the Russian sources were so important that the embryo Minister of Supply in early seventeenth-century England, John Tradescant ('garnetter' to the Crown), made a voyage there and reported in 1618 that the inhabitants were speedy and skilful in the use of tools (Allen, 1964).

Setback

Such relations, however, received a setback when the English parliament restrained Dokhtourov, the Russian ambassador, from going to Oxford in 1645. In retaliation the Tsar cancelled the privileges of English merchants and, when King Charles was executed, expelled them all. Into their place stepped the Hanseatic League and the Dutch Traders, as well as native Russians. When Charles II was restored to the throne he sent the Earl of Carlisle to Moscow in 1663 with a retinue of some eighty staff in all. But the delays he met with, recently and delightfully described by John Jolliffe (1967, p. 217ff.), were not conducive to success. By 1669 there were only two English merchants left in Moscow, and the Muscovy Company itself had shrunk to a dozen or so members from the original two hundred-and-one (Anderson, 1954, p. 143ff.).

England's need for naval stores became so pressing, and further outlets for English merchandise so necessary, that determined efforts were made to strengthen contacts. A permanent envoy was sent from England to the Russian court in 1704, and trade grew rapidly. From 13 tons in 1714, bar iron imports to England rose to 1,085 tons in 1728 and to 15,000 tons in 1750. In 1727, 2,812 masts for naval ships were imported from Russia as opposed to 219 from the American colonies (Reading, 1938, p. 30). Associated with such replenishing of British naval requirements were the merchants, such as Muir (at Memel), Pierson and Thornton (at Riga) and Tooke (at St Petersburg).

In 1734 a proper trade treaty was signed. As a result of such trade, some of the Russian nobles acquired the kind of wealth enjoyed today by Arabian sheikhs. But the general impression of Russia was poor. As the diarist, Sir Francis Dashwood, noted: 'perhaps there is no Country, where the Papas (or Priests), not even in England, get drunk so frequently as in this country' (Kemp, 1959-60, p. 211). He reported an English shipbuilder, Henry Nye, as waiting upon the Tsar and seeing 'a hundred and fifty bleeding heads, just cutt off, that lay before the door of a little wooden house, where the Tsar was. Perhaps, says the Tsar to him, the world may think me a Tyrant for this, but did I not act in this manner I should be quickly as one of these' (ibid., p. 212). In the field of science, Russian scientists participated in the international co-operative efforts and correspondence that was so characteristic of the eighteenth century—as Carol Urness shows in her edition of the letters between P. S. Pallas, the Russian explorer, and the Englishman Thomas Pennant (1967).

The first 'county schools'

One Anglo-Russian merchant was Jonas Hanway. Son of a victualler for the navy, he spent some seven years in Russia as a partner in the trading firm of Charles Dingley, for whom he made an overland journey to the Caspian Sea. Upon his return to England, this restless and zealous man sought an outlet in schemes for better roads and pavements, the reclamation of prostitutes and foundlings, the registration of the indigent and regulation of child labour. Dislike of being at the mercy of nature and the elements led him to devise an umbrella and to carry it round with him.

His former partner in Russia, Charles Dingley, suggested in 1753 that steps should be taken to secure better sailors for the mercantile marine (Hutchins, 1940, p. 78). This, he argued, would help alleviate a problem which then, as now, was much in the minds of reformers: the need to channel the energies of turbulent adolescents (a need made explicit by the Bow Street magistrate). Three years later in 1756, on the outbreak of the Seven Years' War, Hanway formed the Marine Society, with a director of the Russia Company, John Thornton, as its treasurer. An important task for the Society was to find naval kit for landsmen volunteers or neglected boys. In the first seven years some 10,000 boys and men were kitted-out at a cost of £23,500; a large bequest by a Hamburg merchant (reduced after litigation to £17,000 in stock) helped in this. When another war broke out, this time against the rebellious American colonists, the Marine Society was revived to assist another 16,000 boys and men. To ensure that the value of this experiment should not be lost, Hanway proposed that each county should establish 'free schools' to teach 'husbandry and manufactory' as well as 'the theory of common seamanship' to boys. More important, he suggested that a variety of useful aids should be provided—land to till, and a rigged ship on which to practise.

At first Hanway suggested that from 100 to 150 acres of waste land would be needed for every 100 scholars. Their several masters would consist of two petty officers, a husbandman, a ploughman and a manufacturer who, when 'there is no work to be done in the field, or bad weather prevents them sailing a ship', should 'furnish them with such employment as best suits their abilities' —like spinning, weaving or clothmaking—'and give a monthly report on them to the Captain' (ibid., p. 76). This must be the first complete blueprint for a labour school; 'complete' since it contained not only architectural plans and a detailed curriculum, but even the words and music for the songs that the boys were to sing. Numbers 26 and 27 of these songs were 'Hearts of Oak' and 'Rule Brittania'. Could human engineering at that time go further? The title of the 'Hanway Plan' was as formidable as the bulky leather-bound folio volume in which it was issued—*Proposal for County Naval Free Schools to be built on Waste Lands giving such effectual Instruction to Poor Boys as May Nurse them for the Sea*

Service. Teaching them also to cultivate the Earth that in due time they may furnish their own food: and to Spin, knit, weave, make shoes etc. with a view to provide their own Raiment, while good Regulations and Discipline diffuse a moral and religious Oeconomy through the Land (1783). It is worth making a trip to the British Museum to see this most detailed scheme, together with a letter in Hanway's own handwriting.

Hanway also deserves credit for the novel idea that the counties should be responsible for such 'regular oeconomical establishments of such *useful instruction*'. The idea, he said, 'became my guest with the news of peace. I gave it the best apartment in my heart' (ibid., p. iv). Moreover, he envisaged that counties should be stimulated by 'legislative authority' to set up a subscription to supplement their own efforts. But his plan was not well received. One critic, Edmund King, F.R.S., suggested that poor boys were better trained on a ship than on land. Hanway replied in *Observations on the Proposal of Edward King* (1785) that the experiment might be tried at first in a few counties so that others could profit from their mistakes. But too ill to fight further, and crippled by bladder pains, he died in the following year, having offered his body for dissection. Just before he died the Marine Society adopted King's proposal and bought an old naval ship capable of housing from 50 to 100 boys, moored it between Deptford and named it the *Marine Society*. But the idea of the 'county school' was to travel through a good many generations before it was anchored in reality.

Hull Trinity House School

It was apt and significant that Hanway's ideas should find a ready hearing at the East Riding port of Hull, then rapidly developing as a port trading with the Baltic.

There, Hull Trinity House was so impressed by Hanway's treatise (a copy of which can still be found in their care), that in 1787 it founded a school, Hull Trinity House School, which was the first technical school in the town. A friend of Hanway's, a Mr Harneis, presented the headmaster, for wear on formal occasions, with an opal ring that had once belonged to Hanway.

Magnet for talent

Analogous to an underdeveloped country today, Russia afforded scope for many Britons to rehearse and develop their skills in a native laboratory. Russian ailments enabled English doctors from the time of Edward Browne (the son of the author of the *Religio Medici*) to that of Sir James Wylie, to establish a system of medical education there. Russian rivers tried the skill of English engineers such as John Perry, whose experience on the Volga-Don canal later helped him drain the Thames from the flats of Dagenham. The Russian army enlisted Scots like Patrick Gordon who helped drive the Turks from the Ukraine, and James Keith who became a Russian general. Other Scots such as Samuel Grieg and the Scottish officers he recruited in the years after 1764 virtually created the Russian navy which, under another, Elphinstone, destroyed the Turkish fleet in the Mediterranean and would have attacked Constantinople if permitted. (This victory enabled Russia to acquire a kind of protectorate over the Christian subjects of the Sultan by the Treaty of Kutschuk-Kainardji in 1774). Even the British Prime Minister, Lord Chatham, confessed himself 'quite a Russ'. Ten years later Russia annexed the Crimea and built an arsenal at Sevastopol.

The tutor-companion to a young Englishman making the Grand Tour—which in this case included Russia—observed:

Perhaps no country can boast the space of a few years, such a number of excellent publications on its internal state, natural productions, topography, geography and history; on the manners, customs, and languages of the different people, as have issued from the press of the academy ... and it may not be an exaggeration to assert that no society in Europe has more distinguished itself for the excellence of its publications (Putnam, 1952, pp. 270-1).

As an 'anticipation' one might place it beside *The Russian Prophecy A Poem, Occasioned by a Remarkable Phenomenon in the Heavens Observed in Russia, February 19, 1785* (published in Sheffield by Gales and Norton, 1787), in which the unnamed poet forecast of Russia:

> Where 'er She wings her tutelary way,
> Arts, Wealth, and Commerce follow in her Train;
> With science shed their humanising Ray,
> And with their Sun-bright Lustre mark her Reign.

Of the gallery of Anglo-Russian merchants two stand out. St. Petersburg-born J. J. Angerstein transformed an association of private underwriters into Lloyds of London and collected what is now the nucleus of the National Gallery. William Langton of Liverpool helped establish the Manchester Society for the Promotion of National Education in 1833.

A historical perspective to all this and more was given by Joseph von Hamel, a member of the Imperial Academy of Sciences, who came to England in 1814 to report to his government on English arts and sciences. For some thirty-eight years he wrote extensively on the history of British science, and, indeed, published in the year the Crimean war broke out, an account of Tradescant's scientific voyage to the White Sea; which we have already noted at the beginning of this chapter (p. 3).

2
Spiritual affairs and national instruction

John Brown's enthusiasm for state church control

The notion that 'Great Britain might be reformed in Russia' was tenaciously held by a vicar of Newcastle-on-Tyne, John Brown. A puritan, who is said to have closed the gaming tables at Bath after a stirring sermon, he considered that 'the two great engines of power by which all reformations are to be accomplished' were 'the unlimited sovereignty and power of her Imperial Majesty' and 'the Greek Church'. He had won the nickname 'Estimate' for his criticisms of English education in his *Estimate of the Manners and Principles of the Times* (1757), and had followed this up with the plea that schools and colleges should be run by the State, which should not allow parents to educate their children 'according to the caprice of their own fancy'. He insisted that 'private freedom of the infant is not *violated*, but only *directed* to its best end, by early and salutary instruction' (Hans, 1961-2, p. 230).

Brown's advocacy of state controlled schools was sharply criticized in England by the dissenter, the chemist Joseph Priestley. Priestley objected because his co-religionists were excluded from both schools and univer-

SPIRITUAL AFFAIRS AND NATIONAL INSTRUCTION

sities unless they conformed to the Anglican Thirty-Nine Articles. But the Empress Catherine approved of Brown's idea of a state church and she invited him to visit Russia as an advisor. Brown was delighted. He looked forward with rapture to 'civilization and a rational system of Christianity extending themselves quite across the immense continent, from Petersburg to Kamschatka'.

> I can fancy (he exuberated) that I see them striking further into the more southern regions of Tartary and China, and spreading their influence even over the nations of Europe; which, though now polished, are far from being truly Christian, or truly happy. Nay I am sometimes fanatic enough to say with Pitt, that as America was conquered in Germany, so Great Britain may be reformed in Russia (Hans, 1961-2, p. 233).

Given an advance of £200 and the promise of £750 more, he made preparations to launch his great project, only to be struck by rheumatism and gout. So, on the advice of friends, he wrote to Catherine II asking her to send about twenty-five young Russians aged ten to eleven to England each year for a four-year stay in schools, followed by a university course. Though Brown's hopes of reforming Great Britain in Russia were cut short by his death late in 1766, he had, at least, stimulated Priestley to write an *Essay on the First Principles of Government* against his proposals. In the meantime, the first Russian translation of Locke's *Some Thoughts Concerning Education* was made in 1760, and its rational, utilitarian approach to schooling was further spread by Count S. Vorontsov who, from 1785 to 1832, was the Russian ambassador to Britain. Both the Count and his brother (who had also been an ambassador to Britain, from 1762 to 1764) played important parts in diffusing Lockean utilitarian ideas throughout Russia.

THE RUSSIAN INFLUENCE ON ENGLISH EDUCATION

Benthamite laboratory

When Catherine the Great embodied these ideas in her *Statute of Popular Schools* (1786), and set up provincial directors of education to superintend the functioning of two new types of school (one type in provincial capitals and the other in district towns), another Englishman promptly set out for Russia. This was Jeremy Bentham whose brother, Samuel, was the technical assistant to Catherine's favourite nobleman. Jeremy was vastly impressed by his brother's technique of building ships, and while there wrote a series of letters on a Panopticon, or Inspection House— a kind of rotunda housing a management complex, with a series of spokes (cells or classrooms) radiating from it. Thus, from a Russian shipyard came a blueprint for an English school. Bentham himself acknowledged that by going to Russia he learned:

> ...what the human powers are capable of, when unfettered by the arbitrary regulations of an unenlightened age; and gentlemen may say what they please, but they shall never persuade me that in England those powers are in any remarkable degree inferior to what they are in Russia (Mack, 1962, p. 403).

'He returned from Russia in 1788 a puffer, radiant with new hopes, determined to put utilitarianism to use' (ibid., p. 402). He offered to build a panopticon in Paris. He even set up a small scale model on his own dining room table and invited the public to inspect it.

At the turn of the century, Bentham was arguing that the state could 'cause this or that portion of Knowledge to be produced and diffused, which, without the demand for it produced by the government, would either not have been produced, or would not have been diffused'. He supported his brief by reference to the Russian educational reforms at that time, which he described as:

> ... an illustrious and more useful example, because more needful, as well as more extensive than all those English ones put together, supposing the execution to correspond with the design (Stark, 1952, pp. iii, 337).

What Bentham called the 'universities and other education-establishments now setting on foot in the Russian Empire' (ibid., p. 338), included a ministry and new French-type universities at Vilna, Moscow, Kharkov and Kazan, with state scholarships and maintenance grants for their students. Bentham's reservations about the scheme were justified, for he noted that its base (i.e. the parochial schools) was weak, and that no provision was made for the serfs.

Bentham's passion for classification and organization also led him to argue that 'a new spring for morality, a new source of power for the laws, an almost infallible precaution against a multitude of offences, especially against every kind of fraud' would be provided if, like English sailors, everyone carried their family and christian names upon their wrists, and noblemen had their titles imprinted on their foreheads (ibid., p. 557). Once more he drew on his brother Samuel for inspiration. Impressed by the school which Samuel had started for training soldiers and their children, in which the teacher was helped by pupils acting as monitors, he published an educational manifesto, *Chrestomathia* (1816). Few of those who know the present-day garish precincts of Leicester Square realize that there, but for the opposition of the shopkeepers in 1817, a Russian-style ideopolis, oriented to science and technology, might have been built. Though this ideal was not fulfilled it long haunted Bentham's disciples.

An idea of Bentham's that his disciples were able to

popularize was that of a meritocracy based on examinations, as outlined in his *Constitutional Code* (1827). This proposed a state-organized 'Examination Judiciary', under a Minister of Justice, which would supervise free competition for Civil Service posts. All questions were to be known beforehand and selected by lottery. The examinations themselves were to be oral. A recent writer has noted a 'strong similarity' of 'some modern Russian examinations' to the proposed Benthamite system (Montgomery, 1965, p. 19).

Certainly, Bentham evoked the admiration of eminent Russian reformers, such as Count N. Mordvinov (later to be the advisor of Tsar Alexander I), who described him as 'one of the first geniuses who have done and do most for the happiness of mankind—Bacon, Newton, Smith and Bentham: each a founder of a new science, each a creator' (Simmons, 1935, pp. 94-5).

Partners in propaganda

As a propaganda centre for ensuring a Christian Europe, a 'unity without union' between Orthodox Russia, Protestant Prussia and Roman Catholic Austria, the Ministry of Spiritual Affairs and National Instruction in Russia was created in 1817. Its instigator, the Tsar Alexander I, had been awarded (in 1814) an honorary doctorate of Civil Law by the University of Oxford, the first Russian to be so honoured. He had also inaugurated the Russian Bible Society, a co-operating partner of the British and Foreign Bible Society whose chief proselytizer, the Rev Ebenezer Henderson, had, whilst in Russia from 1805 to 1825, printed the Bible in ten dialects. In 1816 the Tsar gave him a house in the centre of town, situated on one of the canals in the Imperial

SPIRITUAL AFFAIRS AND NATIONAL INSTRUCTION

Gardens. This he used as a mission base for his operations on behalf of the Society, inviting to his receptions both Orthodox and Roman Catholic bishops. Henderson was a power in the land, building some 289 auxiliary and branch missions in Russian alone by 1826 (Gleason, 1950, p. 21).

Another British proselytizer was William Allen, the Quaker. Having met the Tsar in 1814, Allen wished to remedy the illiteracy of what he estimated sometimes as twenty million, sometimes as thirty million Russians (Allen, 1846, pp. 423, 439). He and his Moscow friends (Samuel Stansfield of Sheffield, Alexander Wilson and Walter Jennings) did their best to promote the monitorial system of instruction so favoured by Bentham. Like John Brown, Allen was anxious to reform England in Russia; for the monitorial method was meeting opposition in England from those who 'would prefer that the poor should remain ignorant, unless they could, at the same time, be educated in their particular creed', whereas in Russia 'these impediments do not exist, and her present enlightened Emperor has it in his power to set the world an example' (ibid., pp. 251-2).

Four young student teachers were sent to England in 1816 under the supervision of the Russian embassy and placed in the care of James A. Heard, who taught them English. Three years later they returned to Russia via France, Switzerland and Germany to train others in the Central Pedagogical Institute. On behalf of the British and Foreign School Society, James Heard had established a monitorial school on the estate of Count Romanoff and, before he died on 28 September 1875, had pioneered in the teaching of the Russian language, writing *A Practical Grammar of the Russian Language* (1827) and *A Key to the Themes Contained in Heard's Russian Grammar* (1840). He also translated Oliver Goldsmith's

Vicar of Wakefield into Russian for use in Russian schools. His work in Russia has recently been exhaustively examined by Hollingsworth (1966) and Zacek (1967).

Allen did more than flex the sinews of the British and Foreign School Society in Russia; he brought back to England the idea of 'social engineering'. His social experiment in Sussex might well have owed something to the 'mir', or village communities, in Russia. Finding the village of Lindfield, near Brighton, to be 'half a century behind' (ibid., p. 385), he and some others bought it and built a 'colony' of cottages and a school. These were so successful that Allen urged other groups to do likewise, and in a pamphlet, *Home Colonies* (1827), argued that such communities generated 'a free and independent feeling' amongst the inhabitants.

The Russian Ministry cited

The Russian Ministry of Spiritual Affairs and National Instruction won favourable comment in England. The Society for the Diffusion of Useful Knowledge, founded at the same time as Allen's Lindfield colony, issued the *Quarterly Journal of Education*. This later praised the Tsar for rescuing Russian education 'from the inefficient hands of a half-informed clergy' by enabling this Ministry to distribute £800,000 annually to seven universities, sixty-four gymnasia and some 150 communal schools, together with a further £600,000 to other educational institutions (vi, 1833, pp. 363-5). The comparison with England was striking, there being no ministry of public instruction and only £20,000 a year being disbursed by the British government.

The *Quarterly Journal* also paid tribute to the ministry's regard for provincial loyalties in Russia: 'the

SPIRITUAL AFFAIRS AND NATIONAL INSTRUCTION

establishments for education in the various parts of this heterogeneous empire have each their individual character, which depends on the origin and character of the various peoples who form the mass of the nation, and on the faith which they possess' (iii, 1832, p. 25). 'The Russian government [it said] has done honour to itself, by the zeal with which it has laboured to promote the education of its subjects; and the prodigious advances which they have made within a comparatively limited period, shew that it has not laboured in vain' (i, 1831, p. 33). Citing as worthy of emulation the opening of public and university libraries in every province (where possible) for mechanics and artists on certain days, (x, 1835, pp. 372-3), the *Quarterly Journal* pointed to the creation of a new Russian class of traders and intellectuals who were exempt from military service, from capitation tax and corporal chastisement (iv, 1932, pp. 169-70). Significantly, the *Quarterly Journal* praised the creation of a School of Civil Engineers at St Petersburg for the training of surveyors for Siberia (ibid., p. 374); as we shall see in Chapter 5, Siberia was of great significance for British India.

Yet the darker side of Russian autocracy was also exposed—the existence of only sixty-three newspapers (and those in twelve different languages) (vi, 1833, pp. 363-5); the censorship (viii, 1834, p. 165) and the serfs (viii, 1834). And though the *Quarterly Journal* described the way in which the six university districts (Moscow, St Petersburg, Kazan, Kharkov, Vilna and Dorpat) ran the education in their areas, it also printed the criticism of Serge Poltoratzsky that 'all that has been published on this subject is very inexact and incomplete' (i, 1831, p. 193). Students were treated 'like schoolboys' (ibid., p. 31), whipped (p. 37), whilst 'no professor would speak out freely' (ibid., p. 30).

THE RUSSIAN INFLUENCE ON ENGLISH EDUCATION

From the St Petersburg marshes to Hampshire

One of Allen's friends, a Sheffield seed-merchant and farmer, was invited to reclaim the marshes round St Petersburg. In the ten years between 1818 and 1828 he drained 100,000 acres of waste and marshland and brought 5,000 of these under cultivation, starting imperial farms at Ochta (1818-1828) and Shushari (1828-1831). His assistant in this was George Edmondson who, on returning to England, founded at Blackburn a school which was equipped with a printing press, a turning lathe, carpenters' tools and bench. He moved to open another school at Preston (Tulketh Hall) where his reputation led to an invitation from the disciples of Robert Owen, who were then organizing a community experiment at Queenwood Hall in Hampshire, to take over its school (Thompson, 1955, p. 247). Edmondson accepted in 1846, only after Robert Owen had withdrawn from the experiment, having no doubt previously heard from William Allen that Owen was a difficult man to work with.

Queenwood College was a seedbed of scientists. Five of Edmondson's staff went on to take chairs (Edward Frankland to the first Professorship of Chemistry at Owen's College, Manchester; John Tyndall to the Royal Institution in London; T. H. Hurst to the Chair of Pure Mathematics at University College, London; H. Devus to that of Chemistry at the Royal Naval College of Science in Ireland in 1874). One of his students became a powerful advocate of free compulsory secular education —Henry Fawcett, M.P.

The problem-solving approach to the curriculum at Queenwood, where pupils 'learned their science in the laboratory and lived in a thorough atmosphere of research' (Thompson, 1955, p. 251), influenced a clergyman at nearby King's Somborne, who had started a school for agricultural labourers. This was the Rev Richard Dawes, whose *Suggestive Hints towards Improved Secular Instruction, Making it bear on Practical Life* (1847) owed much to the visits made by Tyndall and Frankland to his school. Edmondson also visited his school 'from time to time' whilst two King's Somborne boys worked in the College chemistry laboratory for two days a week (Stewart and McCann, 1967, p. 131). Such collaboration survived Dawes's preferment to the Deanery of Hereford in 1850, where he took the opportunity to argue for more competitive examinations.

Benthamites were on the march. But the remorseless logic of their cause needed a little fire and spirit, ignited by mass meetings and national assemblies; and here some help was to be involuntarily given by, of all people, exiles from Russian Poland.

3
Polish exiles

The first wave: 1830

'There has been lavished upon Poland more false sentiment, deluded sympathy and amiable ignorance than any other subject of the present age.' So argued Richard Cobden in his tract on *Russia* (1836). He thought that Lancashire, Yorkshire, Cheshire and Staffordshire could, with their skill and industry, 'combat the whole Russian empire'. Whatever policy of territorial aggrandizement that Russia followed in Persia or Turkey, he was sure that England (as represented by those four counties) would be even more successful if she 'persevered in her present career of mechanical ingenuity'. To the enhancement of that 'mechanical ingenuity' through better educational facilities, Cobden bent his energies, especially in the late forties, when he formed the Lancashire, later, the National Public School Association. He deplored the English habit of making foreign topics a matter of passionate, earnest and internal politics and suggested that such demonstrations did 'more than anything else to consolidate the power of the Russian empire just at the time when it was in danger of being thrown into discord and confusion by the emancipation of the serfs' (Bright and Rogers, 1903, p. 48).

Cobden was criticizing those who campaigned in this country on behalf of Poles exiled in England after their revolt against Russia in 1830. The campaigners, in turn, argued that the cause of the Poles was that of the English crusaders for the ballot and the abolition of the Corn Laws. Thus the *Westminster Review* held:

> If the Russians are driven over the Niemen we shall have the Ballot; if they cross the Dneiper we shall be rid of the Corn Laws... Poland is God Almighty's granary; it is the place where ought to be grown the millions of quarters of corn, the thousands of millions of quartern loaves, which should be dropping into the mouths of children who are starving... Poland has its liberation to win and so have we... and we cannot do better than carry on the contest in concert (Gleason, 1950, p. 132).

English liberals like Thomas Campbell, one of the founders of the University of London, and Sir Thomas Wyse, the eminent Irish educationalist, had joined forces to form local pro-Polish groups in places like Hull, Manchester and Birmingham. Poland's cause was Britain's: rights were rights, no matter where the battle was being fought. The president of the Society of Friends of Poland founded, in 1835, the *British and Foreign Review* which became an anti-Russian organ, whilst other journals such as *Polonia* and *The Hull Polish Record* concentrated on 'the cause'. Among the exiles of 1830 was the chief of the Department of the Polish Ministry of Public Instruction, Count Walerjan Krasinski. He had established a Jewish college in Warsaw, and now he turned his hand to writing on Slavonic themes for the Society for the Diffusion of Useful Knowledge, his articles for their *Penny Encyclo-*

THE RUSSIAN INFLUENCE ON ENGLISH EDUCATION

paedia in 1841 and 1842 being amongst the earliest of such popular expositions. His friend, Lord Dudley Coutts Stuart (who obtained £10,000 from Parliament for the relief of Polish exiles on 10 August 1835), supported his scheme in 1844 for a chair of Slavonic studies at Oxford (Simmons, 1952, p. 137). So did William Fox-Strangeways, who, as the fourth Earl of Ichester, later endowed such teaching there in the person of W. R. Morfill.

The second wave: 1851

When further Polish and Hungarian refugees arrived in Liverpool in 1851, a committee was formed to find work for them in the North. Some went to Newcastle where they were assisted by the wealthy young Joseph Cowen, who began to devote himself to the Polish Democratic Society in London. He helped smuggle agents into Poland, financed the export of arms and propaganda, and, during the Crimean War, issued a new periodical, *The Northern Tribune*. This voiced the revolutionary sentiments of the Polish friends for whom he was organizing meetings. Other people organized Foreign Affairs Committees in the large industrial towns, believing that there was a collusive conspiracy between the British and Russian governments against the rights of man.

Polish emigré societies made history at this time; with French and German emigrés and the rump of the Chartists they formed the first, if shortlived, International Association of Working Men (Brock, 1958/9, p. 119).

The most distinguished exile of this generation was Alexander Herzen who, during his stay in London between 1852 and 1865, contributed regularly to English journals. His friend, W. H. Dixon, was the editor of the *Athenaeum*, whilst he himself started the Free Russian Press in the Caledonia Road, writing an account of it for the readers of the *Saturday Review*, 27 June 1863. Herzen's opinion that Communism was the destined future of Russia had a considerable impact (Partridge, 1962, p. 453ff.). Carlyle told him in 1855 that he would 'much prefer Tsarism itself, to the sheer Anarchy (as I reckon it sadly to be) which is got by "Parliamentary eloquence", Free Press and the counting of heads' (Carr, 1933, p. 371).

The third wave: 1863

But it took the Polish revolt of 1863 to encourage further efforts for the 'good old cause' of the ballot. Edmond Beales, President of the newly formed Polish National League and Chairman of the Circassian Society, used these societies to agitate for English as well as for Polish self-determination. This became clear when the Polish aspect of the agitation died down and the societies joined the trades unions to form a national pressure group, known as the Reform League, under Beales's presidency. In mass assemblies, notably that of 23 July 1866 in Hyde Park, they pressed their case until the passage of the Reform Bill in 1867 gave them the vote and the ballot, and posed the further problem of educating those who were to use the vote. This problem had been especially posed by the consequences of British participation in a war against Russia, at which we look in the next chapter.

4
The aftermath of the Crimean War: 1854-1867

Essential expertise

Creeping into Siberia and establishing settlements on its southern boundary, Russia loomed, ever more menacingly, over the Northern frontiers of India. Wellesley saw this and urged the East India Company to establish a college at Fort William. But the Board of Directors turned down his proposal in 1800. When the Russians established, in 1810, the Institute of Ways and Communications to train engineers for Siberia, the East India Company had to reply, and did so in 1813 by establishing two colleges—one at Haileybury for administrators, and the other at Addiscombe for engineers. Like its Russian counterpart, Addiscombe was virtually the only English institution training engineers for service in underdeveloped areas. From this time on Englishmen, often in disguise, clambered up the Himalayas to penetrate the dangerous buffer zones in Central Asia, only to find Russian agents also busy at winning friends and influencing people.

As an oceanic power, Russia's potential was, in the opinion of Sir William Symonds, Surveyor of the Royal Navy, well based on the new naval college at St Petersburg,

AFTERMATH OF THE CRIMEAN WAR: 1854-1867

where 'scientific officers' were trained. Visiting it in 1839 he noticed the numerous 'objects for experiments in galvanism and other branches of chemistry; and an ingenious table for the purpose of attaining the art of manoevring ships and fleets' (Sharp, 1858, p. 223). Symonds was especially impressed by the 'great abundance of instruments' and 'a great many students' at the Hydrographical Office.

Visiting Sevastopol in 1841 he was moved to write

A system somewhere they have found,
In principle and practice sound,
By which they most excel us.
These Muscovites a knack have got,
To find what's right and what is not,—
A plodding set of fellows. (Sharp, 1858, p. 283).

Twelve months later his intimations were to be confirmed.

Having blown the Turkish fleet out of the water at Simope in 1853, the Russians initiated, in the war that followed, a series of technological changes. Against the greatest amphibian operation of the century, they devised an ironclad steam-ship and mines to defend Cronstadt. To defend Sevastopol their able engineer, Todleben, devised a system of sand-bagged, interconnected trenches that enabled him to hold off the British and French for eighteen months. So bad were conditions in the British Expeditionary Force that the British government fell. From the filth and confusion of Scutari, 'calamity unparalleled in the history of calamity', according to Florence Nightingale, a new ethic and practice of nursing emerged. To prevent other British armies being destroyed, she urged the reform of the army Medical Department. Her *Notes on Matters Affecting the Health, Efficiency and Hospital Administration of the British Army* (1858) laid the emphasis on efficiency. A Military Medical College (at

Chatham in 1859), the first military hospital (at Woolwich in 1861) and a permanent army sanitary commission (in 1862) resulted from her campaign.

Competence vs cousinhood

The administrative muddle revealed by the Crimean War was intensified by the campaign to replace cousinhood by competence as a qualification for appointments. Sir Charles Trevelyan (who was, as the assistant secretary to the Treasury, deeply concerned with the commissariat and supply arrangements for the Crimea) had been, with Sir Stafford Northcote, involved in an inquiry into the means whereby this could be affected in the Civil Service. So passionately did Trevelyan feel that patronage imperilled the country that he described 'the infirm, incompetent generals' as 'covering our name with disgrace and increasing the horror of war a hundredfold'. He pointed out that 'our people are few compared to the multitudes likely to be arrayed against us, and we must prepare for the trial by cultivating to the utmost the superior morality and intelligence which constitute our real strength' (Hughes, 1949, pp. 69-70). The impact of the Crimean disasters, following on the appearance of his and Northcote's commission in 1855, led the Prime Minister to establish the Civil Service Commission by order in Council in that year.

The Civil Service Commission exercised an enormous influence over English education—as Trevelyan had intended, when he told Gladstone:

> Among the many benefits of this plan, there is none which I contemplate with so much gratification as the effect it is likely to have in giving our Rural Population a motive to educate their Children, thus bringing the Standard of cultivation in the country nearer to a level

AFTERMATH OF THE CRIMEAN WAR: 1854-1867

with that in the Towns, at the same time that religious and moral training are more attended to owing to the more perfect carrying out of the Parochial System in the rural districts and to the influence and exertions of our Country Gentlemen and Clergymen and their Families. At present the Standard of Education in the country districts is lamentably low. A few days since, finding myself in Company with several country Gentlemen and Clergymen in Somersetshire, I asked them how many young men they supposed there were in their respective neighbourhoods who would have a chance of carrying off the prize for the inferior class of appointments—and after some reflection and discussion, they replied scarcely any except a few Farmers' sons. The boys almost always leave the National Schools at 11 or 12 years of age to pick stones or keep birds. Instead of being overwhelmed with candidates, therefore, we shall be at a loss for them as far as the rural population is concerned (Hughes, 1949, pp. 210-211).

Trevelyan's visit to Somerset stimulated the Bath and West of England Society for the Encouragement of Agriculture, Arts, Manufactures and Commerce to form a small committee to organize a local examination for schoolboys. Prizes were put up for competition. The first examination was held at Exeter in 1857; subsequent ones were sponsored by Oxford as 'local' examinations. These developed into the complex system of school certificates known today as the G.C.E.

The war and popular education

To consider the state of the army before Sevastopol a committee of inquiry was appointed by Parliament. It was a therapeutic for its members, who came to appreciate the need for efficiency in the services. Sir John Pakington, an ex-minister of war, was especially impressed by this need. On 16 May 1855 he introduced a bill which made provision for a system of popular education through boards—castigated by one of the leaders of his own party as 'the secular system in disguise' (Hansard, 137, col. 685). Yet to Pakington it was 'by far the most important and most pressing of all the questions of the present day, affecting the safety and welfare of the institutions of the country'.

William John Fox, the advocate of previous bills for promoting popular education, pointed out that the illiteracy revealed by the Crimean War had highlighted the necessity of the bill, for the troops at Scutari were, for the most part, unable to read the tracts distributed amongst them (Hansard, 137, col. 686). Pakington introduced yet another such bill in February 1857. When that failed he moved for the appointment of a Royal Commission on Popular Education in 1858. This time he was successful, and indeed secured a place on the famous Newcastle Commission, which stressed the need for efficiency and system.

As if to emphasize the lesson Victorian Britain had to learn from Russia, Pakington, now Secretary of the Navy, was responsible for the announcement that two iron-cased ships—*Warrior* and *Black Prince*—were to be built for the fleet. Pakington returned to the attack in May 1864 asking for a committee of enquiry into the constitution of the Committee of Council itself (Hansard, 175, col. 382). He repeated the demand in February 1865, describing the Committee as inefficient and irresponsible (Hansard, 177, col. 848). He won both his point and the appointment as chairman of a Select Committee on Education. In his draft report he argued (1866, p. xvi) for a 'Minister of Public Instruction who should be entrusted with the care and superintendence of all matters relating to science and art and popular education in every part of the country.'

AFTERMATH OF THE CRIMEAN WAR: 1854-1867

The rise of B.S.A.

On the outbreak of the Crimean War the fourteen firms called upon by the government to supply arms formed themselves into an association called the Birmingham Military Arms Trade. As their chairman, J. D. Goodman held office from 18 January 1855 till he died in 1900; and under him they became the Birmingham Small Arms Company in 1861. With his fellow townsman, Sampson Lloyd, managing director of the bank of that name, founder of the Birmingham Chamber of Commerce and chairman of the United Kingdom Chambers of Commerce, Goodman went to Russia to the fifth National Exhibition of Arts and Manufacturers held in Moscow, with a view to repairing the ravages of the Anglo-Russian trade caused by the war. They found that the importation of British goods was 'no longer a profitable or honest occupation' (Michell, 1866, p. 563).

Equally depressing was the picture of Russian social life given by the annalist of London's poor, Henry Mayhew. 'Travelling from England', he remarked, 'is like going backward in time—every ten degrees of latitude corresponding to about a hundred years in our own history'. This was especially true of Russia where he found 'a state of villainage and serfdom exists almost at this day, as it does with us in the feudal time of the conquest' (Mayhew, 1864, p. ix).

The military and Russia

In 1867 a deputation of English artillery officers visited Russia. It was impressed by 'a particularly good model of a horse which took to pieces' and the Russian army chemical laboratory, which it described as 'superb'. The delegation also noted that 'great importance' was attached by the Russians to 'general education', and that the course at the Russian Military Academy was comparable to that given to the advanced class of artillery officers at Woolwich (Turner, Warren and Nolan, 1867, p. 601). Commissions, they pointed out, could be either obtained from the ranks or, as *junkers*, on graduating from the military schools (Artillery, Engineer, Cavalry and Infantry, plus the School of Pages and a military school at Moscow). They heard 'many of the officers speak well certain tongues', and though attributing it to 'family background', thought it worth comment.

Their opinions were reinforced by those of another army officer, Colonel Alexander Strange, who had returned to England six years earlier after extensive service in India (where he had established a department for the inspection of scientific instruments). Elected Fellow of the Royal Society, and its foreign secretary, Strange now became convinced of the need for state aid 'to secure the progress of physical science'. He read a paper on the subject to the British Association in 1868; this had such an effect that a Royal Commission under the Duke of Devonshire was appointed in 1870 to consider the matter. Its eighth Report recommended that a Ministry of Science and Education, with a Council of Science, should be established to foster such instruction.

5
Nihilism and science

Bazarov: the embodiment of nihilism

'Is your special study physics?' Bazarov is asked in Turgenev's *Fathers and Children* (1862). He replies 'Physics, yes; and natural science in general' (Garnett, 1926, p. 40). But he went further: 'A good chemist is twenty times as useful as any poet' (ibid. p. 42). And throughout the rest of the novel Bazarov speaks as the voice of empiricism, the dethroner of principles, or, as he is called early in the story (p. 35) a nihilist. This was a term with which the English were to become familiar. By 1871 the *Annual Register* (p. 226) defined it as 'an offshoot of Russian extravagance on the Socialist stock'. The metaphor was too patronizing. Nihilism really stood, as Turgenev's English translator pointed out, for *'the sceptical conscience of modern science'* (the italics are hers, used on p. xiii); and Bazarov, its formulator, represented to her *'the bare mind of Science first applied to Politics'* (p. xii). As far as readers of the *Fortnightly Review* were concerned, the type was accurately described as early as 1868 in an article on 'Nihilism' by Borborykin, who described them as passionate devotees of the study of natural sciences and believers in objective investigation as the only way of arriving at knowledge and truth.

The 'completely unexpected news' that Oxford was going to award him the 'Doctorate of Natural Science' astonished Turgenev in 1879, for this degree was actually a Doctorate in Civil Law. He was even more surprised when he went to receive it in the June of that year. For, instead of the usual chorus of 'catcalls and hisses' which he expected (because 'they still cannot stand Russians in England') he found himself 'applauded more than the others' (Lehrman, 1961, p. 321). As the first Russian (apart from the Tsar Alexander I in 1814) to be so honoured, Turgenev symbolizes the interpenetration of Russian culture and that of the West. True, his efforts were exerted mainly in France, but it was through the French window that many Englishmen got a view of the richness and variety of Russian life.

G. H. Lewes and his contributors

The editor of the *Fortnightly Review*, Lewes, was himself more than sympathetic to such ideas. He was a positivist and his wife, George Eliot, had translated the work of the German materialist Feuerbach. Indeed the *Fortnightly* was run on nihilist lines—if one accepts Turgenev's definition of a nihilist in *Father and Sons* as 'a man who bows before no authority, who accepts no principle without examination, no matter what credit the principle has'. Its editor had been employed by a Russian merchant in the 1830's before entering journalism, and as editor of the radical *Leader* and the Benthamite *Westminster Review* had persuaded the Russian exile, Alexander Herzen, to contribute to these journals. In the July 1854 number of the latter, readers were told that Herzen believed 'Communism to be the destined future of Russia ... as it lay deep in the people's feelings' (p. 128). When Lewes launched the *Fortnightly Review* in 1856 (as its name implies, a more frequent version of the *Westminster*) he had recruited writers like A. W. Benni and Peter Boborykin.

Another of Lewes' contributors had taught himself Russian, often learning by heart whole pages of the dictionary. This was W. R. S. Ralston, who made a name as a public lecturer on Russian literature. His lectures were so successful that in time he used to fill London halls like St George's and St James' as well as others in the provinces. So well known did he become that Cassells, the publishers, commissioned him to write a book on Russia. But at the last moment he stood down and suggested that Donald Mackenzie Wallace, another contributor to the *Fortnightly*, undertake the task instead. This was a brilliant suggestion for Wallace's *Russia*, published in 1877, became a standard work.

Wallace and the Russian challenge

Wallace showed that the Nihilists developed utilitarian ideas to extremes, as when they argued that a shoemaker who practised his craft was greater than a Shakespeare or a Goethe 'because humanity has more need of shoes than poetry' (Wallace, 1877, p. 157). 'Englishmen may have some difficulty', he wrote, 'in imagining a possible connection between natural science and political agitation ... In Russia it is otherwise ... As soon as they had acquired a smattering of chemistry, physiology and biology, they imagined themselves capable of reorganizing human society from top to bottom.' (ibid., p. 623).

At the same time Wallace showed the two-fold nature of the challenge the Russians offered to England's hegemony in world markets: their skill in colonization, and their determination to emulate England. He described the Russian peasant as possessing:

> a power of self-adaption which we headlong, stiff-necked Britons know nothing of, he easily makes friends with any foreign population among whom his lot is cast. He has none of that consciousness of personal and national superiority which so often transforms law-respecting, liberty-loving Englishmen into cruel tyrants when they come in contact with men of a weaker race or a lower degree of civilisation. Nor has he any of that inconsiderate proselytizing zeal which makes pagans so often fail to recognise in British Christianity the religion of love. Each nation, he thinks, has received from God its peculiar faith, and all men should believe and act according to the faith in which they have been born. When he goes to settle among a foreign people, even when his future neighbours have the reputation of being inhospitable and unfriendly to strangers, he takes with him neither revolver nor bowie knife (Wallace, 1876, p. 147).

On the second point he was more explicit:

> England is at the present time like a great manufacturer who has outstripped his rivals, and has awakened in the breasts of many of them a considerable amount of jealousy and hatred. By means of her ruthless 'politique d'exploitation', it is said, she has become the great bloodsucker of all less advanced nations. Fearing no competition, we preach the invidious principles of free trade, and deluge foreign countries with our manufacturers to such an extent that native industries are inevitably overwhelmed, unless saved by the beneficent power of protective tariffs. In short, foreign nations in general—and some of our own colonies in the number—have adopted, in no friendly spirit, the theory quaintly expressed by the old poet, Waller: 'Gold, though the heaviest metal, hither swims; Ours is the harvest where the Indians mow, We plough the deep, and reap where others sow!' In no country are these ideas more frequently expressed than in Russia. As revolutionary politicians when in opposi-

tion systematically attack all restrictions on the liberty of the press, and systematically adopt these restrictions for their own benefit as soon as they come into power, so the Russians habitually assail with impassioned rhetoric our commercial and industrial supremacy, and at the same time habitually seek to emulate it.

Wallace was, as D. G. Morren has shown (1967), the leading spokesman of the British Russophiles.

Early warnings of Russia's technical intelligentsia

Six English scientists and industrialists were appointed in 1881 to 'inquire into the Instruction of the Industrial Classes of certain Foreign Countries in technical and other subjects, for the purpose of comparison with that of the corresponding classes in this country; and into the influence of such Instruction on manufacturing and other Industries at home and abroad. They described (though they did not visit) the Moscow polytechnic. This, they reported in 1882, gave 'a very high-class engineering education'; and noted that practical work earned up to £10,000 a year for the schools in contracts. Though only sixteen years old, its 'theoretical training' was 'of a very high order, most nearly resembling that of the École Centrale of Paris' (C3171, 1882, p. 205).

Their opinion was shared by percipient Americans who, seven years earlier, had appreciated the pedagogic rather than the profitable aspects of the Moscow polytechnic. For at the Philadelphia Exhibition of 1876, in the words of an American historian, the Moscow exhibit had shown 'for the first time that Russian educators had finally scored a breakthrough on the thorny problem of how to organize meaningful, instructive shop training as an essential adjunct of technical education'

(Cremin, 1961, p.24). This 'breakthrough' was programmed polytechnism: graded practical work done in the apprentice workshops. Two of the percipient Americans who saw this founded counterparts of the Moscow 'shop' at M.I.T. and Washington University, St Louis. Indeed the principal of Washington University, St Louis, argued that such combination of practice and theory in meaningful conjunction was the only way in which 'the productive toiling classes' could be educated beyond the eighth grade. Other types of bookish middle-class education, he contended, actually deterred students from entering industry.

This drive to educate the working classes in Russia intensified when the Russian minister, Uyshnegradski, drafted a 'general plan' in 1884 aimed at replacing foreigners by natives in Russian industry. All posts from manager down to foreman were to be filled by Russians trained in various types of technical schools corresponding to the job. Thus Higher Technical Colleges were to train managers and Trade Schools to train foremen. Both would be recruited from urban or primary schools. Later, under Count Witte, the Higher Technical Colleges were supplemented by three lower types—Intermediate Technical Schools, Lower Technical Schools and Trade Schools. In 1893 Lower Trade Schools and Schools of Apprentices were added. Besides this, various ministries —Agriculture, Ways and Communications, and Finance —ran their own schools. Those under the Ministry of Finance included the Commercial Schools.

Visiting these early in the twentieth century, an English H.M. Inspector described them as 'no inconsiderable achievement', since they prevented 'the waste, over-lapping and want of co-ordination from which English education so frequently suffers' (Darlington, 1909, p. 478). They were aiming at what he described as an impossible ideal, impossible because it implied a higher standard of general education for the working classes than was attained even in the most advanced countries in Western Europe (ibid., p. 472).

The premonitions of Seeley and others

If Russia emulated Germany in the organization of the educational system, and if it completed its railways, Sir John Seeley prophesied that with the United States it would 'surpass in power the states now called great as much as the great country estates of the sixteenth century surpassed Florence' (Seeley, 1884, p. 301). His only remedy was to suggest that English colonies should be made 'part of England'. Nor was Seeley alone in his fears, for Sir Charles Dilke forecast in *Problems of Greater Britain* (1889) that France and Germany would be pygmies compared to Russia when her strength was developed. So Sir John Seeley preached the gospel of imperial service to students studying history and law at Cambridge, where a teaching revolution was taking place, private coaches being replaced by officially appointed college tutors.

Another Englishman, J. Cartmel Ridley after attending the International Geological Congress held at St Petersburg, wrote that Russian museums suggested to him 'how much might and should be done in this direction in many of the county towns of England for the mental elevation of the people' (Ridley, 1898, p. 78). He was also impressed by the electric lighting in Nijni Novgorod and wished that English municipal authorities should do likewise (ibid., p. 87). He urged that 'English people should certainly travel in foreign countries more than they at present do. This would certainly tend to open the eyes of many who at present are apparently oblivious of the fact that we have most watchful and far-seeing competitors' (ibid., p. 100).

Five years later, Albert Beveridge, a distinguished American historian travelling in Russia, noted that 'technical schools of various sorts are springing up throughout the empire. Frequently you will run upon some special institution for learning, such as the University for the Study of Oriental Languages at Vladivostock. In Blagavestchensk, Siberia, a neat little structure was pointed out as a school of riparian navigation. And Russians contend that their military schools, and particularly one institution of this kind, are the most perfect in the world. The common schools are fairly numerous too. Strange to say they are more numerous in Siberia, in proportion to the population, than in Russia itself' (Beveridge, 1903, p. 423).

A year later, H. J. Mackinder read a paper to the Geographical Association (which he had helped to found) on the 'Geographical Pivot of History'. The 'pivot' as he saw it was the northern and interior parts of the Eurasian continent—this he called 'the Heartland'. Re-worded and revised over a number of years he summed it up in a proposition:

> who rules East Europe commands the Heartland; who rules the Heartland commands the World-Island: who rules the World-Island commands the World.

The War office again

Russian technological development of Siberia and Central Asia continued to excite the suspicions of the War Office which, in a *Survey of the Military Resources of the Russian Empire* (1907), stated that:

> the purpose underlying Russia's patient and methodical advance and her vast expenditure upon unremunerative

railway construction is obvious; without necessarily intending to conquer and absorb our Indian Empire, she aims at eventually making her frontier and that of India coterminous, or at least bringing it so near that she may be in a position to strike effectively if Great Britain should, as in 1878, venture to thwart her policy (Williams, 1966, p. 365).

The War Office was shrewd, as subsequent events showed. Russian industrial growth between the years 1885 to 1911 was 5.72 per cent per annum as opposed to 2.11 per cent in the United Kingdom. It was also greater than that of Germany (4.49 per cent) or America (5.26 per cent). Indeed, from emancipation to 1900, Russian industrial production increased more than seven times, whereas in Germany it increased five times, in France 2.5 times and in England barely doubled (Gerschenkron, 1947, pp. 144-174).

Darlington's Report: 1909

By 1909 the Department of Special Inquiries and Reports published the most authoritative plea up to that time for learning from Russian centralization. For 'the English system (if so it can be called)', it said, 'with its lack of cohesion, its unco-ordinated aims, its bewildering variety of curricula, its untrammelled freedom of instruction, and its traditional tendency to treat education as a private concern' (Darlington, 1909, p. 356), was by no means necessarily superior to that of Russia. For whereas the English system was 'little more than a temporary commission for giving legislative effect to reforms demanded by the community,' the Russian contained a permanent built-in impetus, with public opinion playing a role 'not unlike that of the opposition in a constitutional state'.

THE RUSSIAN INFLUENCE ON ENGLISH EDUCATION

As Darlington saw it, Russian-type centralization had several advantages. First, it 'facilitated a general reform of education whenever this is thought desirable by the government', whereas in England 'enormous difficulty' was encountered 'even when such alteration is shown to be a matter of urgent national importance'. Second, since universities and schools were part of the Russian state system, it was possible to look on education 'from a broad national standpoint', whereas in Britain public schoolmasters and dons were 'not so much members of a profession as members of particular societies within a profession'. Indeed, he found no English counterpart to the interest diplayed by Russian universities and secondary schools in primary schools. Third, he noted that, in Russia, education always received a good press. There was keen public competition for university places, which were allotted on merit. The *attestat zrelosti* (or entrance requirement, established in 1863), was an examination he described as having a 'higher average attainment in classics, mathematics and the mother tongue than is required for admission to most British universities'. Even the Oxford and Cambridge standard, which might exceed it, did so only 'at the cost of a specialization in the curriculum which most Russians would consider very undesirable' (ibid., p. 361).

Darlington unfortunately died in 1908, the year before his magisterial study was published. His massive report to the Board—some 569 pages—was salted and peppered with shrewd asides on the relevance and meaning of Russian educational policies. Of particular interest was his opinion that 'the Russians have no intention of letting another century or more go by before their country takes the place in the industrial world to which its vast natural resources and the native capacity of its people entitle it' (Darlington, 1909, p. 496). 'Nor would they look on England as a model, for their belief in education as a factor in industrial progress, tended', he pointed out, 'to turn their eyes to Germany and Japan'.

Russian science in England

Meanwhile, in England, there had been developing a real respect for the contributions of Russian scientists. This virtually began with the homage paid to D. I. Mendeleev, the Siberian chemist, for his work on the physical constants of chemical compounds. 'No man in Russia', wrote the English chemist T. E. Thorpe in 1889, 'has exercised a greater or more lasting influence on the development of physical science...and...nowhere has (his) pre-eminence been more quickly recognized than in this country'.

This last is also true of the most contentious educational idea of our time: conditioning. Although it was originated by the Russian physician Sechenov in 1863, the idea gained popularity through the work of a professor at the Military Medical Academy on the secretions of the glands, especially the digestive glands of dogs. In 1900 Pavlov's famous experiment on a dog became the classic illustration of the 'conditioned reflex'. He was elected F.R.S. in 1907 and awarded the Copley medal in 1915, and his work was translated into English in 1902 by W. H. Thompson.

Russia established the Laboratory of Experimental Pedagogy in the museum of the Ministry of War. Three years after its first director, A. Netschajeff, took office in 1901, he established a special pedagogical institute and, within another three years, post-graduate courses for intending teachers. A Society of Experimental Pedagogy was formed in 1908, together with an Institute of Psycho-neurology in Petrograd (1907) under Bekhterev and an Institute of Child Psychology and Neurology (1912) under Rossolino. Short courses and conferences were organized in experimental education in 1906, 1908, 1910 and 1913, whilst Netschajeff organized the manufacture and circulation of small psychological 'cabinets' to more than a hundred schools or pedagogical societies throughout Russia. These cabinets contained, amongst other things, a tachistoscope for testing pupils' reactions. One such cabinet came into the possession of Professor J. A. Green of Sheffield University, who founded and edited the *Journal of Experimental Pedagogy* (now the *Journal of Educational Psychology*) to which he asked both Netschajeff and Rossolino to contribute.

Behind these two loomed the greater figure of Bekhterev who, as we have seen, founded the Institute of Neurology in 1907. Stimulated by Pavlov he tried to show how psychic processes were linked to physiological functions. So devoted was he to this work that he coined for it the name reflexology, rather than psychology. His work on conditioned motor reflexes (associated reflexes) even envisaged a physico-chemical explanation of psychological or biological behaviour. On the social significance of such ideas Bekhterev was very vocal. Not only child growth, but labour, suicide, crime and other social problems fell within his orbit, and after the revolution he applied his theories to the general problems of Soviet planning. But not until 1933 was his work translated into English, by which time Soviet planning itself had become better understood.

Russian exiles: Kropotkin and his friends

One of those who wrote resumés of foreign, especially Russian, science for *Nature*, *The Times* and the *Newcastle Chronicle*, was Prince Kropotkin, who first came as an exile to England in 1876, returning ten years later to stay until 1917. During these thirty years in England he founded the Freedom Press with Mrs Charlotte Wilson and Dr Burns Gibson. He enjoyed the company of such scientists as H. W. Bates, Patrick Geddes and John Scott Keltie, and anarchists, including Joseph Lane, Ambrose Barker and Henry Seymour. Indeed, he is credited with converting Philip Snowdon (later a Labour Minister of the Crown) to Socialism.

Together with his wife he became a popularizer of current science, writing some seventeen papers on various topics (for example the rise of X-rays) for the *Nineteenth Century* between 1892 and 1901; whilst she delivered popular lectures on biology and chemistry in Surrey. At their homes in Harrow, then Acton, Bromley, and Muswell Hill, they entertained such popular science writers as Edward Clodd and Grant Allen. Kropotkin told Edward Clodd that:

> So long as three quarters of the education of this country is in the hands of men who have no suspicion of there being such a thing as scientific (inductive and deductive) thinking, and so long as science herself will do everything in her power to preach most absurd and unethical conclusions, such as 'woe to the weak', then all will remain as it is (Woodcock and Avakumovic, 1950, p. 256).

He also told the Teachers' Guild in 1893 that they could 'not eschew the necessity imposed upon them by the development of science, industry and civilization as a whole, of educating children in natural sciences in the proper way'. By this he meant physics as taught in France, atomic energy and geography as in Germany and student exploration as in Russia.

> I do not see (he argued) why, during the Easter holidays, the boys of a London school wishing to visit the Lake District, could not go and hang their hammocks in some

school building in Cumberland for the holiday week... the amount of valuable materials gathered by the boys of the upper classes of the secondary schools, and especially by the pupils of the teachers' seminary of Caucasus, as well as by such as have the chance of staying in remote and unexplored mountain districts, can be seen from the excellent year books recently published by the School Administration of Caucasia (Kropotkin, 1893, p. 8).

Kropotkin did his best to remedy the unethical nature of Darwinism by his *Mutual Aid: a Factor of Evolution* (1902). This tempered the abrasive individualism of Darwin's 'struggle for life' by citing the facts of animal life as he had found them in his explorations of Siberia. He also gave a certain elegance to anarchism of a Communistic kind, writing an article on the subject for the *Encyclopaedia Britannica*. His numerous articles on geography, intensive agriculture and anarchism were slanted to the future, showing that machines would soon provide so much leisure that men would undertake work on the land to restore their equilibrium. He forecast the neuroses engendered by men's iron slaves, and saw that the intensive use of the kilowatt hour would encourage decentralization.

Other members of the Russian 'book club' who found refuge in England were its founders, Nicholas Chaikowsky, Sergius Stepniak and Felix Volkhovsky. Sergius Stepniak (or Sergei Mikhailovich Kravchinsky as he was called in Russia) was well known in English radical circles where his novel, *The Career of a Nihilist*, was issued by the Walter Scott Publishing Company in 1890. His pamphlets were issued five years later with an introduction by that doyen of North-Eastern Liberals—Robert Spence Watson. Spence Watson considered nihilists to be 'miscalled', as they had the same desire as English liberals to 'lay aside all matters which are not absolutely essential, and of working closely and unitedly together for these fundamental objects which all alike hold dear' (Stepniak, 1895, p. ix). As one of the founders of the College of Science (now the University of Newcastle), a keen anti-Sabbatarian, and a member of the Newcastle School Board, Spence Watson was alive to the potentialities of the Zemstvos, or Russian county councils, and formed with Felix Volkhovsky in 1890 the Society of Friends of Russian Freedom. The Society published *Free Russia* for which, over the next twenty years, Spence Watson wrote a number of articles. Support was also given by Liberal M.P.s like Thomas Burt and William Byles and by that indefatigable tract writer Hesba Stretton (Miss Sara Smith), whose *Readings for Working Men* and religious tracts made her one of the guardians of the collective conscience of late Victorian England.

To support the revolutionary movement in Russia a Parliamentary Committee on Russian Affairs was organized in 1908; the Bulletin it sustained was edited by Volkhovsky and David Soskice, a translator from the Russian, whose son Frank later became a Labour Home Secretary.

The fifth wave: the Jews

Meanwhile the Russian government was progressively curtailing the freedom and personal security of the Jews. From 1890 it began to expel them wholesale from Moscow, Kiev and other cities. A Russo-Jewish Committee of distinguished Englishmen was formed; this addressed a memorial to the Tsar in 1891 (which he refused to accept) protesting against the persecutions, which reached their height during the Russo-Japanese War of 1904 and the Revolution of 1905. So many Jews sought refuge in England that the British government tried to control the flood with the Aliens' Act of 1905. Neither this nor the apprehensions of Major Evans-Gordon could check the flow, which by 1911 had brought 106,082 'Russians and Poles' to England and Wales. Apart from the large numbers in London, so many went to Manchester that its Jewish population increased from 5,000 in 1865 to 28,000 in 1900.

The contributions of these Jews were considerable. Amongst the immigrants was the distinguished chemist Chaim Weizmann, who devised the 'doping' of wings of aircraft in the First World War. The second generation included Sir Lewis Namier (to whose writings the new conservatism owed much), Harold Laski (a formidable exegete of pre-Wilsonian Socialism) and Silig Brodetsky (who did much for mathematics at Leeds University). Grandsons of the immigrants include David Daiches of Sussex University and John Yudkin, the nutrition expert at Queen Elizabeth College. The catalogue would be incomplete without Sir Jacob Epstein the sculptor, Solomon the pianist, and Sir Leon Bagrit the pioneer of automation.

Nor, as immigrants in a country which was once described as a 'nation of shopkeepers', should the contribution of Michael Marks—a refugee from Russian Poland in the early 1880s—be forgotten, for at Leeds he started with Tom Spencer a chain of penny bazaars. They were joined after the First World War, by the son of another Russian emigré from Lithuania, Israel Sieff. Sieff's scientific and empirical skills, learned from a third Russian-born emigré, Chaim Weizmann, transformed the chain of penny bazaars to the present firm of Marks and Spencer, whose trade mark, St Michael, has often been described as the badge of an affluent society. Sieff's part in another distributing agency—this time of ideas

—will be explored in Chapter 9. That agency was P.E.P.—Political and Economic Planning.

There was one macabre by-product of this unhappy period in Russian history. To convince the Tsar Alexander II that there was an Israelite plot against him, the Russian government manufactured evidence. The chief of police found a satire on a Russian Minister (Witte) and with the help of a monk called Nilus fabricated the notorious *Protocols of the Elders of Zion*. This forgery was later brought to England by another waves of exiles—this time White Russian officers in 1919. It alarmed the *Morning Post* and provided, for a time at least, an excuse for some absurd anti-Semitic feelings, and not a little hostility to the Revolutionary Government of Lenin.

6
Ecumenical efforts

Epiklesis vs economics

The invocation, if not the influence, of Russia is almost as old as Anglicanism, since *epiklesis* (or the invocation of the Holy Spirit upon the bread and wine) in the first English Prayer Book of 1549 was derived from the Eastern liturgies.

Clergy such as Bishop Andrewes, the seventeenth-century bishop of Winchester, and Isaac Basire, who held a Chair of Divinity in a Transylvanian university, were strongly attracted by these liturgies.

Later Anglicans, who had refused to take the oath of allegiance to William III, proposed to the Russian Holy Synod and the Eastern Orthodox Patriarchs that they should adopt a common prayer and liturgy and establish a common church in London to be called Concordia. Another suggestion, which got further off the ground, was a college to train preachers and schoolmasters for the East. Benjamin Woodroffe persuaded the Levant Company to refurbish Gloucester Hall, at Oxford, then a disreputable ruin, to house students from the East who would train as interpreters for the Levant Company. Of the few who came from Greece, three ran away to

Paris, and others migrated to Halle; the Levant Company withdrew its help in 1704 and the Orthodox Church placed a veto on further students.

A third scheme was put forward by the author of the first Russian grammar to be published in England, H. W. Ludolf (Simmons, 1950, p. 104), who proposed that an 'Oriental College' be founded. His *Proposal for Promoting the Cause of Religion in the Churches of the Levant* in 1712, envisaged it as providing instruction in 'the Eastern Language' (ibid. p. 147). Forty-two years later someone suggested that if his idea was put into action in London it would 'strike as great a panic upon our avowed enemies at home and abroad, as his Majesty's respectable fleet' (ibid., p. 5).

Holy Russia

The headmaster of Rugby, Thomas Arnold, confessed to a friend in 1840 that he could 'not help looking to Russia as God's appointed instrument for such revolutions in the races, institutions and dominions of Europe, as He may yet think fit to bring about' (Stanley, 1890, p. 395). Arnold's view was shared by the Rev James Long, who went to India for the Church Missionary Society in 1846. Long was a vigorous advocate of Russian 'good intentions', having spent his early life there. In subsequent visits in 1863, 1867 and 1876 he detected what he called a 'thawing process' which would enable the Russians, with Britain to Christianize Asia. He lamented that 'Russia has in former days been too much described by pens dipped in Polish ink; happily there is a great revolution in English opinion of late years' (Long, 1874, p. 4). This 'revolution' was an increasing appreciation of Russia as a democratic country where fraternity and equality flourished under the feeling of great loyalty and reverence to the Tsar.

Arnold's pupil, A. P. Stanley, also went to Russia, and through his writings made Englishmen even more familiar with the Orthodox Church; especially with the views of the remarkable Philaret, Metropolitan of Moscow. Philaret, who served on the Synod of the Orthodox Church for forty-six years (1812 to 1867) is credited with the authorship of the Tsar's manifesto freeing the slaves in 1861. His ecumenical ideas had been made available in English by a member of the British and Foreign Bible Society, Robert Pinkerton. To Philaret, faith was the bond of the invisible church. The visible (and weak) churches could not, therefore, stigmatize as false any other church based on the faith that Jesus was Christ.

Ecumenism as well as *epiklesis* began to stir in Victorian England. Some even thought that the Russian Church would be an effective ally against the Roman Catholics. Certainly some Russians encouraged them to think so.

In 1840 William Palmer went to Russia and asked to be admitted to Holy Communion. By this he wished to demonstrate the unity of the Church: but his act was appreciated neither by his brother Anglicans nor by the Orthodox Church. The chief procurator of the Holy Synod (a layman and a cavalry officer, Count Pratasov) considered him 'strange and frivolous', and Orthodox monks also found him so 'heretical' that (they told him) they refused to pray for the Anglicans. But Palmer made a Russian friend who considered that England had more in common with Russia than any other country in Europe. Both countries had a sense of community. Both were basically conservative civilizations. Both were essentially religious and anti-rationalist. Described as 'the first original theologian of the Russian church' (Zernov, 1944, p. 56), this friend, Alexei Khomiakov (a layman, ex-Guardsman and mathematician), lamented the discipline, intolerance and compulsion of the Roman Church which had led to the growth of individualism and rationalism. Papalism and Protestantism were to him progressive stages towards this. But the Russian Orthodox Church was democratic; it did not accord the hierarchy with the guardianship of dogma and rites, but regarded all its members as collectively infallible. Khomiakov also applauded the English passion for emptying the streets on a Sunday.

The Eastern Church Association

Palmer's trip was not in vain, for when he left Russia in 1842 he was told by Count Pratasov that a new chaplain would be appointed to the Russian church in London. This was the Rev Eugene Popov, who came in 1843 and stayed for thirty-two years. Popov was a remarkable man. He made friends with Pusey and Newman and with the erudite John Mason Neale, to whom he taught Russian so successfully that Neale was able to undertake a masterly investigation into the rites, doctrines and hymns of the Eastern church. Some of the latter were included when *Hymns Ancient and Modern* was first published in 1861, and others appeared in the *English Hymnal*.

From his researches, Neale became 'thoroughly convinced that the Latin doctrine is grievously erroneous, suspected of heresy, and even (if logically carried out) heretical' (Lough, 1962, p. 126). His *Voices from the East: Documents on the Present State and Working of the Oriental Church*, translated from the original Russ,

Sclavonic and French, with Notes (1859) marked an impressive stage in the dialogue between the two Churches. The Metropolitan of Moscow sent him a copy of the Liturgy of the *Starovertzi* (Old Faith dissenters) with an inscription.

Popov and Neale founded in 1863 the Eastern Church Association, in which venture they were supported by H. P. Liddon who, five years later after a visit to Russia, wrote that the 'Sense of God's presence—of the supernatural'—seemed to him 'to penetrate Russian life more completely than that of any of the western nations' (Johnson, 1950, p. 100). The Eastern Church Association was revived in the 1880's by W. J. Birkbeck, an enthusiast for Russian plain-song. With Bishop John Wordsworth of Salisbury (an original founder) he tried, but failed, to establish postgraduate scholarships at Oxford and Cambridge to train graduates for service in Russia. Birkbeck became such an authority on Russia that he was chosen to accompany Lord Kitchener there during the First World War. Lord Halifax wrote to him:

> I don't think anyone in the world has done more than you have to make Russia known to the West, and the West to Russia, and how good it is that you have been able to keep foolish people in order, who try to go too quick, and make proposals to Russia that anyone who knows anything about the country knows they could not and would not accept (Birkbeck, 1922, p. 301).

Birkbeck was a particular friend of K. Pobedonostsev, the Chief Procurator of the Holy Synod, who tried to counter the 'atheising' tendencies of the Zemstvo schools by establishing a system of church schools. By 1893 Pobedonostsev had slowed up the growth of Zemstvo schools so that they numbered only 13,280 (with 910,587 pupils), whilst his own church schools numbered 31,835 (with 981,076 pupils). Yet the Russian Zemstvos did help church schools with grants—the very solution which the Anglican Church was advocating in England, and which the 1902 Act was to secure.

New forms of religious experience

However much some Englishmen might court the Orthodox Church, there was no denying that its musical record was poor, indeed, orthodox zealots had once tried to proscribe the use of musical instruments. But the steady rise of the technocratic spirit in the 1860s led to the formation of a group known as the 'mighty handful', consisting of Tsezar Kui (a distinguished military engineer), Borodin (a chemist), Stasov (a lawyer), Balakirev (a mathematician), Mussorgsy (an army officer) and Rimsky-Korsakov (a naval cadet). This group hoped to rescue Russian music from its servitude to Italian models by cultivating a realist, one might even call it a religious approach to music. Similar trends were later displayed in the Russian theatre, where H. A. Meierhold hoped to adapt the techniques of the church to that of the stage by concentrating on moving the 'soul' of the audience. This pervasive movement in the arts spread to the novel, which the Russian writers like Tolstoy and Dostoevsky were to use with powerful effects in England, as we shall now see.

7
Tolstoy and his English exegetes

Yasnaya Polyana

Having founded a school on his estates at Yasnaya Polyana in 1859, and following this up with a journal bearing the school's name, Count Leo Tolstoy wrote to the nihilist Chernyshevksy: 'the journal and the education of the peasants mean everything to me' (Hans, 1962, p. 93). Chernyshevsky replied by urging Tolstoy to get on the level of contemporary science, but Tolstoy insisted that he was not so much concerned with training (*vospitane*) as education (*obrasovanie*), which schools and universities virtually prevented. Science, he argued, could only be imparted by people who love it.

Tolstoy's *Childhood and Youth*, first translated into English in 1862, excited what Edmund Gosse called a vain and capricious agitation' in England (Gosse, intro., 1890). But vanity and capriciousness were not the animating motives of those Englishmen who hailed Tolstoy as the Moses who would lead people plagued by extreme division of labour and increasing specialization out of the festering cities of 'Egyptian' England. As Havelock Ellis said: 'Tolstoy, with his semi-oriental quietism has returned to the rationalistic aspects of the social teaching of Jesus' (Ellis, 1890, p. 219). Tolstoy preached of work, fraternal love, self-denial and self-mastery. And as W. T. Stead, the most dramatic publicist of the age, proclaimed: 'Here, in the heart of Russia, has arisen a teacher who stood at the summit of the culture of his generation and proclaimed, in strange new accents, the old-world message, Ecce homo!'. Like Arnold, Stead held that 'the next great wave of religious revival that would influence European development would take its rise in Russia' (Stead, 1888, p. 405).

Discipline, and with it formal grammar, history and geography, did not exist at Yasnaya Polyana. Instead pupils explored and exploited areas of their own imaginative experience. They learned to read by the liberal use of pictures, but if they could not, no attempt was made to force them. Not to argue an 'ism' is to argue alone, and Tolstoy could be included under no particular banner. His *The Alphabet of the Social Sciences* (1871) was attacked in what Mikhailovsky later called *A Storm in a Teacup of Pedagogic Water*, and he was summoned to Moscow to defend his system of teaching reading. Later, as his great gifts unfolded, he renounced the Russian Orthodox Church and came to believe that the Kingdom of Heaven was within every man. Through his novels—parables rather—he made such an impact that Matthew Arnold remarked in 1877: 'The Russian novel is now the vogue and deserves to have it. If fresh literary productions maintain this vogue and enhance it, we shall all be learning Russian'.

Tolstoy and Matthew Arnold

Matthew Arnold had met Tolstoy in 1861, when Tolstoy had come to England to look at schools with a view to gathering ideas for Yasnaya Polyana. The meeting impressed Tolstoy more than it did Arnold. He liked Arnold's idea of 'detaching the good from the bad' by means of disinterested criticism, if only to prevent the retarding effects of the Scriptures. He especially warmed to Arnold's idea of 'destroying the notion of God as something outside us, a "magnified man"'. To him, God was 'that endless eternal principle, which is outside us, leading us, demanding righteousness of us' (Mainwaring, 1952, p. 274). In his turn Arnold described Tolstoy's *What I Believe* (1884) as containing 'sound and saving doctrine' even though it went farther than he, Arnold, would go. Tolstoy, he argued, would cause a revolution. And Tolstoy in turn was moved to castigate Arnold's cultural quietism, so typical of Europe 'with its Krupp guns, smokeless powder, journalism, strikes, constitutions and Eiffel Tower'.

It was apt that Arnold's essay on Tolstoy should first appear in *The Fortnightly Review* of December 1887 (pp. 783-799). Though a long resumé of Tolstoy's *War and Peace* had been given to readers of the *Nineteenth Century* by W R. S. Ralston in April 1879 (pp. 650-669), Ralston thought that its length (and that of *Anna Karenina*) 'among other deterrents' would prevent it being translated into English. The *Saturday Review* had also enthused over it (LXIII, 1887, pp. 22-23). But Arnold 'had a special reason for writing about Tolstoy'; as he told a friend on 24 February 1888, it was because 'of his religious ideas'.

The English Tolstovitsi (i) the colonies

These 'religious ideas' won Tolstoy many English disciples. One was Edward Carpenter, whose criticisms of modern science (which enabled governments to become, in Herzen's well-known phrase, 'Genghis Khans with telegraph systems') so aroused Tolstoy's admiration. Tolstoy's son, Sergei, translated Carpenter's *Modern Science: a Criticism* (an essay which Carpenter later republished as part of a better-known work, *Civilization: its Cause and Cure*, 1889), and Tolstoy himself wrote a preface for it. Like Tolstoy, Carpenter had also rejected institutional religion (he had once been a curate) and had settled, in 1878, in the Derbyshire hills near Sheffield. Here he subsisted on a small holding like a peasant for over forty years, during which time he became a virtual 'guru' to local radicals. To this day his house is a place of pilgrimage for older members of the Labour Party. Like Tolstoy, Carpenter was to be, with his brother, a moving spirit in the formation of a school in the country. It was originally to have been sited near his own cottage at Totley, at the foot of the Derbyshire hills; but the availability of property elsewhere led to it being established at the other end of Derbyshire, at Abbotsholme. Carpenter was a friend of that other peasant craftsman, George Sturt, and of the pioneers of the ill-fated 'simple-life' colony financed by Ruskin at Totley, and of another colony, inspired by Tolstoy, a mile or so away at Norton (Armytage, 1961, pp. 293-301, 310-312).

In accordance with Tolstoy's dictum that the essence of educating children was to educate oneself, several other social experiments in the form of 'simple-life' colonies were undertaken in the last decade of the nineteenth century. Like their Russian counterparts, the English *Tolstovitsi* were uncompromisingly opposed to state power, war, and organization. At one of them, Whiteway near Stroud, the colonists even burnt the title-deeds to their land as a symbol of its conveyance to the Real and Eternal Owner. At another, Purleigh in Essex, Tolstoy's most intimate Russian disciple, Tchertkov, helped the Doukhobors' emigration from Russia to Canada. Tchertkov's activities in England were connected with the publication of Tolstoy's works. He virtually took over the Brotherhood Press (which had hitherto been issuing translations of some of Tolstoy's more inflammable pamphlets) with the help of A. C. Fifield, and renamed it The Free Age Press. They took a building at Christchurch in Hampshire which they surrounded with a barricade, and all visitors were scrutinized through a loophole in it before being admitted (Schuyler, 1928, p. 217).

The English Tolstovitsi (ii) the cells

But the real personality amongst the English *Tolstovitsi* was Aylmer Maude. He had lived in Russia for twenty-three years, first as a pupil, then as a tutor and finally as a business man. Here he had become a great friend of Tolstoy. Though by no means wholly in agreement with Tolstoy's teaching, he and his wife nevertheless settled for a time at the English colony at Purleigh in 1897, and when it broke up four years later they became Tolstoy's main translators and literary expounders in English. Tolstoy authorized Maude to write what has become a standard biography, and after Tolstoy's death he set about the publication, in twenty-one volumes, of all Tolstoy's writings. As he pointed out, Tolstoy's importance lay in his emphasis on self-education. He considered that Tolstoy had stimulated W. T. Stead to start the World's Classics Series. This series was bought out by one of Stead's assistants, Grant Richards, who subsequently sold it to the Oxford University Press (Maude, 1911, p. 209).

Dismal Manchester, 'a workhouse with a brick wall round it', was the centre of a most lively Tolstoy group. Its leading member was Percy Redfern who (having read the socialist futures pictured by Bellamy and Morris, and flirted with agnostics, secularists, republicans, Malthusians and others who thought there should be no God, no King and as few people as possible) encountered Tolstoy's writings in 1899. 'I feel,' he wrote, 'a problem solved. Tolstoy haled me forth. He laid hold of the life I knew and interpreted it' (Redfern, 1946, pp. 49-50). So the Manchester Tolstoy Society began with lectures by Aylmer Maude (Tolstoy's English translator) and Vladimir Tchertkoff (his chief 'agent' in England). Since it was not 'anti-' anything, its members enriched the ranks of The Society of Friends, Adult Schools, the Unitarian Church—and even the Anglicans. For as Redfern says, 'into organizations not professedly religious, it sent individuals to work with hope and confidence in the meaning of life for themselves and their fellow men' (ibid., p. 99).

Similar 'cells' were formed in Blackburn, where a school on the Yasnaya Polyana model was opened in a labourer's cottage. In Derby, William Loftus Hare edited the most attractively designed of all the Tolstoyan journals: *The Candlestick*. Like them, it uncompromisingly rejected 'the Establishment', publishing articles which urged the liberation of education from state control. Certainly the sage's most industrious exegete in England, Aylmer Maude, wrote in 1911: 'a radical stand such as Tolstoy has been able to make throws all such efforts as that of Settlements into the ugly light of compromise and inefficiency—at least so it seemed to me—and perhaps accounts for a certain defensive account I found in myself' (Maude, 1911, p. 526).

The intense vein of religiosity in Tolstoy, which inspired followers like the editor of *The Candlestick*, also inspired the Rev Walter Walsh, a minister in Newcastle and Dundee, who confessed:

> not only did he (Tolstoy) show me the miserable incompetence of orthodoxy but he unfolded the ethical content of religion in a way that filled my mind with

enthusiasm, and led me to see that the unity of mankind might be reached through the unity—not the uniformity —of religion. I believe that Tolstoy saved me from the lamentable mistake of secularising my career (Walsh, 1921, p. 18).

Walsh derived the message that 'it was not enough to provide for the coming of God's Kingdom. We had to *organize it*' (Walsh, 1921, p. 19); and in *Jesus in Juteopolis* he described the plight of inhabitants in Dundee so graphically that he was made chairman of the Town Planning Committee. In 1913 he succeeded Charles Voysey as 'pope' of the theistic church, terminating his ministry in 1916 to concentrate on this.

D. H. Lawrence and his friends

One faithful register of an Englishman's reactions to Tolstoy was a young graduate of the University College of Nottingham, who was teaching in 1911 at Davidson Road Secondary School ('a fine red place—new and splendid!') at Croydon. He told one girl friend to 'read Balzac, Ibsen and Tolstoy and think about them' (Moore, 1962, p. 138), and another to 'read *Anna Karenina*—no matter, read it again, and if you dare to fall out with it, I'll—I'll swear aloud' (ibid., i, p. 54). But when, five years later, this young teacher, now well known as the novelist D. H. Lawrence, came into contact with such Futurists as Marinetti, he found Tolstoy's moral scheme 'dull, old, dead' (ibid., p. 281). Disenchantment led him to regard Tolstoy, Turgenev and Doestoievsky, de Maupassant and Flaubert, as 'obvious and coarse'.

Lawrence's progressive disenchantment with Tolstoy was soon replaced by a passionate interest in the Revolution of 1917. 'I feel', he wrote to his friend

Koteliansky—a Russian exile in England, 'that our chiefest hope for the future is Russia. When I think of the new young country there, I love it inordinately... We will go to Russia. Send me a Berlitz grammar book, I will begin to learn the language—religiously (ibid., 1962, p. 513).

Lawrence was a diffuser of Russian ideas. He wrote:

> Russia seems to me now the positive pole of the world's spiritual energy, and America the negative pole... How can I write for any Russian audience?—the contact is not established. How can the current flow when there is no conviction. As for England, it is quite hopeless (ibid., i, p. 516).

And again: '...Russia will be righter, in the end, than these old stiff senile nations of the West' (ibid., i, pp. 562-3).

With Lawrence, as translators of Russian authors, were John Middleton Murray, Katherine Mansfield and Virginia Woolf, the last-named the most elegant spokeswoman of the middle-class nationalist intelligentsia of her day. Her admission that 'out of Shakespeare' there was 'no more exciting reading' than Dostoievsky, shows that another Russian gospeller was at work in England; his novels, she said, were 'composed purely and wholly of the stuff of the soul... hot, scalding, mixed, marvellous, terrible, oppressive' (Woolf, 1933, pp. 226-8). In the same year (1859) that Tolstoy founded his school at Yasnaya Polyana, Dostoievsky had returned from four years exile in Siberia as a convinced Christian. Horrified at the 'indescribable darkness and horror' being prepared for mankind 'under the guise of renovation and resurrection' he warned his contemporaries that security and prosperity were making men afraid of freedom. He predicted a conflict between Christian and anti-Christian forces and believed that the Orthodox Church would have a vital and mediating role to play in the working out of the dilemma.

The Garnett circle

With Tolstoy, Turgenev, Chekov, Gogol and Herzen, Dostoievsky was translated into English by Constance Garnett, a service which led Katherine Mansfield to tell her: 'My generation and the younger generation owe you more than we ourselves are able to realize ... These books have changed our lives, no less. What could it be like to be without them!' (Heilbrum, 1961, p. 166). Constance's husband, Edward, was no less active as a publisher's reader; at Unwin's, then Heinemann's, John Lane's, and finally at Jonathan Cape's, he played a major role in the development of the English novel, and achieved some literary immortality as Bossinney in *The Forsyte Saga*. He discovered not only John Galsworthy, but D. H. Lawrence as well, and Joseph Conrad, son of a 1863 'exile' from North Russia.

Constance Garnett was the first librarian of the People's Palace, an educational and recreational centre built by Sir Walter Besant for the Cockneys, Jews and foreigners of Whitechapel. Herself having links with Russia as the grand-daughter of the naval architect to Tsar Nicholas I, she met Russians such as Kropotkin, Volknovsky and Stepniak. Stepniak persuaded her, whilst she was going through a difficult pregnancy, to learn Russian, and subsequently induced her to publish her first translation—Goncharov's *A Common Story*. The two Garnetts played a vital role in disseminating Russian ideas in every department of English life. One of her friends, who had fled from Russia, was Joseph Fels, who devoted the fortune that he made from his famous naptha soap to social reform movements. He, in turn, was an especial friend and supporter of George Lansbury, the labour leader.

And Lansbury was to be one of the most likeable defenders of the 'new order' prevailing in Russia after the revolution of 1917.

8
The Red bogey: 1919-1930

The polarization of feeling towards the Soviets

To oppose outside interference in the internal affairs of the U.S.S.R., and to secure the establishment of normal trading relationships, a 'Hands-Off-Russia Committee' had been formed in England in 1917. This secured the support of the Labour Party and the T.U.C. by stressing that the U.S.S.R. had shown that Labour was 'fit to govern.' Ranged behind it was the newly founded *Daily Herald* under its editor George Lansbury, which, from the first number on 31 March 1919, spoke out uncompromisingly for a full peace and friendly relations. Its joint secretaries, W. P. Coates and E. F. Wise, were to be stalwart defenders of the idea that Labour was 'fit to govern'—Wise becoming M.P. for Leicester. In public demonstrations, like that on 27 February 1920, Coates and Wise packed the Albert Hall with people who cheered Israel Zangwill when he asked that if the object of allied attempts to crush the Soviets was 'to keep Bolshevism out of England, why had it not done so?' Similar meetings were promoted by the *Daily Herald* on behalf of George Lansbury.

But many other groups in England denied Labour's

fitness to govern, and for three reasons. First, the Bolshevik defection (which had enabled the Germans to transfer thirty-five divisions from the Eastern to the Western front and inflict well over 120,000 casualties on the British Fifth Army alone) made Englishmen 'see Red'. Subsequent failure to dislodge the revolutionary governments by an ill-timed intervention in no way mitigated their dislike of the new Russia. Second, the Bolshevik dissolution of the democratically elected constituent assembly, in which they held only 175 seats out of 707, was regarded as highly undemocratic. Last, and perhaps most important of all, the repudiation of all foreign investments—in Britain's case some £600 millions—was regarded as a financial and moral outrage.

Three travellers' reports

Of the numerous visits and deputations made by English men and women on Russian achievements in overcoming the fearful obstacles of starvation, illiteracy and lack of trained talent, three were especially noteworthy. The first was that of the well-known children's author, Arthur Ransome, who was extremely impressed by the way in which the Soviets making the best of appalling material difficulties—for example the feeding of children at school, as much to keep them alive as to promote habits of regular attendance (Ransome, 1919, p. 188). He was also impressed by the Consultative Council of the Commissariat of Education. Visiting it for the *Manchester Guardian* on 28 February 1919 he found that it was composed of representatives of various bodies—trade unions, co-operatives, teachers and so forth —and that the Commissar for Education, Lunacharsky, took its advice. Such initiative on the part of councils of soviets had also, he pointed out, led to the establishment of universities and new polytechnics 'to get as many working men into the universities as possible' (ibid., pp. 181-2). Libraries had grown and 'a remarkable organization' had developed for the circulation of printed matter through the post offices. 'The Soviet Government,' he wrote, 'has earned the gratitude of many Russians who dislike it for everything else it has done, by the resolute way in which it has brought the Russian classics into the bookshops' (ibid., p. 186). Ransome pointed to the new technocracy, 'the young engineers in particular', who realized, 'the new possibilities opening before the (textile) industry, the continual need of new improvements, and the immediate welcome given to originality of any kind' (ibid., p. 149). Such sentiments were later to reverberate in Britain. Today he is regarded as one of the shrewdest observers of that time (Mandel, 1968, p. 295).

The second visit was that by the former director of the men's training department at the Victoria University, Manchester, who contrasted the Russia of 1920 with that of 1911, and felt 'almost envious' (Goode, 1920, p. 86). Their 'largeness of vision' he found 'striking', and he detected 'a wave of intense desire for instruction of all kinds' (ibid., p. 83).

A third visitor was that veteran friend of pre-war Russia, H. N. Brailsford. He compared England where:

> ... advanced Liberals spoke of 'the educational ladder' by which they mean a system which will help the more capable children of the manual workers to climb above their class, (but) there is no real attempt to rear the whole mass of working-class children in the best culture of their age.

to Russia where:

> Every fair-minded observer has given the Bolsheviks credit for their prompt efforts to send an illiterate people

to school. Their ambition is much bolder. They intend from infancy to adolescence to make, for every Russian child, the conditions, both physical and intellectual, which will enable its mind to evolve its utmost capacity (Brailsford, 1921, p. 75).

The Trade Union delegation of 1920

A delegation from the British Labour Party and Trade Union Congress, visited Russia in 1920 under the chairmanship of Ben Turner. Its members were Dr Haden Guest, Mrs Snowden, Miss Margaret Bondfield, A. A. Purcell and H. Skinner (T.U.C.) Tom Shaw and Robert Williams (Labour Party), and Charles Roden Buxton as a co-secretary. Haden Guest was very impressed by the schools of Petrograd and reported that one of them (the 27th Soviet School) had a chemical laboratory 'fairly well equipped, and a physics laboratory very well equipped indeed, with all kinds of electrical apparatus and with much mechanical apparatus'. He also noticed that though teachers had signed a return certifying that religious ikons had been removed from the dormitories, 'yet there were still numerous ikons seen above the beds'. When he heard children singing the 'Internationale' at Moscow he found the experience 'oddly reminiscent of English children singing "God Save the King"' (Haden Guest, 1930, pp. 145-6).

'Without being a Communist', wrote Mrs Snowden, 'one could heartily congratulate those who were responsible for bringing so much light and happiness into the lives of men and women for whom those good things had been unattainable in the past' (Snowden, 1920, pp. 100-1). They were far from being 'completely subdued by the dominating Communist passion for disciplined classification and routine', and she found that Lunacharsky, the Commissar for Education, was an advocate of 'Luciferism'—his own word for the habit of challenging authority. The Director of Education for Petrograd was, she discovered, a woman; Mrs Zinoviev. She was the wife of a man whose name was to be distressingly familiar in England four years later.

The Zinoviev letter

Zinoviev was the first chairman of the third International, or Comintern. This dated from the days of the Polish exiles (see Chapter 3), who helped form the first International in 1864. After it died sixteen years later, a second International took shape in 1889, but it also failed at the unattended Proletarian International Congress convened at Vienna in August 1914. Lenin therefore made a third attempt at an International by convening a conference of delegates at Moscow on 4 May 1919. This third International or Comintern was not only opposed to capitalism but to 'reformist' socialism too.

Having come into office for the first time early in 1924, just as signs of an economic revival were visible in Russia, the Labour government hoped to solve the problem of British unemployment by a trade treaty with Russia. But though the Prime Minister, Ramsay MacDonald, became the first Head of State to recognize the Soviet government, his action stirred those who had lost money by the Soviet revolution. The Association of British Creditors of Russia and the Big Five banks wanted the Soviet Union to discharge its debts, to cease propaganda and to restore properties confiscated from foreigners. A figure of £1,040,000,000 was mentioned as the total owed. In reply the Russians cited Russian gold deposited in British banks during the war and damages caused by the British army of intervention.

An Anglo-Russian Conference was held and resulted

in, amongst other things, the promise of a loan from Britain to the U.S.S.R. This was attacked by all the Chambers of Commerce, the F.B.I. and other critics of the government. The attacks were so penetrating that the Labour party, deserted by its Liberal allies, went to the country. Five days before the election the *Daily Mail* dropped a bombshell: a letter purporting to come from Zinoviev, head of the Communist International, urged the British Communist Party to initiate a class war against the opponents of the Anglo-Russian treaties. This brought down the Labour Government (which lost 113 seats) and gave the Conservatives an overwhelming majority. It was ironic that the Zinoviev letter was a forgery by White Russian exiles, abetted by the Polish government (Chester, Fay and Young, 1967, p. 55).

The death of the Liberal Party

Of the three results of the Zinoviev letter two were immediate. The Liberal party was destroyed as a political force by losing over one hundred seats in October 1924, while the British Labour party finally severed its last links with the Communist Party of Great Britain. The third was long-term. Up to its publication Britain had, in the words of the most recent study 'led the gradual process of diplomatic rapprochement with the Soviet Union, giving a lead that found many imitators on the continent'. Afterwards the British Government 'led the diplomatic retreat from Moscow' (Chester, Fay and Young, 1967, p. xvii). The results on Russia were natural. Being isolated, it developed an isolationist mentality. The very failure of subsequent English attempts to prove that the Zinoviev letter was a forgery seemed to intensify the coldness of England's Eastern shoulder.

THE RUSSIAN INFLUENCE ON ENGLISH EDUCATION

The Trade Union delegation of 1924

After the election of 1924 a second delegation from the T.U.C. visited Russia in 1924; it considered that Communism could 'best be understood as a new religious order of devotion and discipline', and the Comintern 'not so much as a publicity department of a political party as a preaching order' (Russia, 1925, p. 12). One of the members, A. A. Purcell, had been in the previous delegation in 1920. The others were the President of the Miners' Federation of Great Britain (Herbert Smith), the founder of the Dockers' Union (Ben Tillett), the founder of the Shop Assistants' Union (John Turner), the General Secretary of the Railway, and of the Society of Locomotive Engineers and Firemen (John Bromley, M.P.), the General Secretary of the United Patternmakers' Association (A. A. H. Findlay), and the General Secretary of the T.U.C. (Fred Bramley). Accompanying them were three other old 'Russia hands'—Captain H. G. Grenfell, R.N., A. R. McDonnell and George Young—who, it is suspected, wrote much of the report.

'Certainly astounding' was their verdict on the educational system. Their deepest impression was of the 'Young Pioneers' whose singing of folk songs seemed to them like 'the wailing cry of a people long oppressed brought into contact with a glimpse of freedom and hope for a better future' (ibid., pp. xii-xiii). They endorsed the emphasis on obtaining qualifications and the training necessary for such qualifications. These afforded 'an entirely new outlook on life and made their leisure hours a pleasure'. The meritocratic nature of the system appealed to them because 'a peasant or a worker could by his own energies rise in his or any other profession with the aid given to him by the system'. They contrasted this with England where talent often lay 'wasted and dormant' and concluded that this 'seems likely to become very rare among the workers of Russia' (ibid., p. 121). The delegates also approved of the system for National Health which 'at the present rate of progress' would set an example to the states at present leading Europe in these matters (ibid., p. 135).

So favourable was the report of the second Trade Union delegation that a group of Labour party members, composed mainly of Kropotkin's old associates such as T. H. Keell (the backbone of the British Committee for the Defence of Political Prisoners in Russia), commissioned another old Kropotkinian, Emma Goldman, to attack it.

The revival of the 'religious question' in English education

When another Labour government, pledged to re-establish diplomatic and commercial relations with Russia, was elected in 1929 under pressure from the T.U.C. (which wished to stimulate Anglo-Russian trade in order to alleviate unemployment), ambassadors were exchanged between Moscow and the Court of St James. But the breach was not to be healed quickly. This time the Russian hostility to religion was queried. For the Russians, believing that there was a link between religion and counter-revolution, had convened a conference in Moscow in 1925 to define the ways in which counter-revolutionary tendencies in religion were to be attacked.

All religious teaching in Russia had already been forbidden by proclamation on 26 October 1917, which also called for the conversion of churches and monasteries into schools, clubs, storehouses or Anti-God museums for exhibiting sham relics and other curiosa. A newspaper, *The Godless* (Bezboznik), was issued in 1922 and a number of anti-God societies sprang into being. A further Soviet decree of 8 April 1929 ordered religious communities to be registered and forbade financial levies on people outside the communities' own membership.

So 'a Christian Protest Movement' took shape in Britain; this was backed by *The Morning Post* which organized huge meetings against Russia in the Albert Hall. The first of these was on the day before the Soviet ambassador presented his credentials. Other meetings followed, and many of the clergy who spoke, from the Archbishop of Canterbury downwards, could turn on the following day to *Morning Post* and the *Daily Mail* to find their sonorous condemnations faithfully reported. But to the Soviet Union it was 'trite stuff... Not even the invented names of would-be religious martyrs in the U.S.S.R.' it replied, could 'lend colour to such incredible ideas. Remembering the oppressive role of the Church under the Tsar, the people of the Soviet make no secret of their dislike for religion, but every visitor to the Soviet Union knows that we fight religion by education and propaganda and not by the methods of the medieval inquisition'. It was useless for the official news agency, Tass, to point out that 'priests who refrain from counter-revolutionary activities are allowed to conduct religious services unmolested', for the Christian Protest Movement now had the bit between its teeth, Prayers were ordered in the churches 'for the persecuted people of Russia' and when the Labour Government forbade these to be used in services, it was described by the *Daily Telegraph* (28 February 1930) as applying 'pure Soviet methods of Government and administration'.

This agitation had one important effect on an educational measure at the heart of the Labour Party's programme—the raising of the school leaving age to fifteen. The proposal, if implemented, would have put a strain on the voluntary schools which at that time they could not have borne. Ironically, the case against the raising of the school-leaving age was moved in the House of Commons on 29 May 1930 by a Labour M.P., John Scurr: ironically because as editor of the *Socialist Review* he had been a leading member of the Hands-Off-Russia Committee. After the second reading of the Bill for raising the school-leaving age had foundered on 29 May 1930, the Christian Protest Movement itself seemed to wane. Its last meeting in the Albert Hall, on 14 July 1930, closed with a resolution urging 'the Soviet Government to give full liberty of religious teaching and worship to the people of Russia', and extending 'to all God-fearing people in that land (its) cordial greetings of sympathy and hope'. These events were watched with such lively apprehension that the Government issued a White Paper on the subject in 1930 (Cmd 3641).

9
Mediators and interpreters

Berdyaev and the Y.M.C.A.

More than any of the million-and-a-half Russians who poured into Western Europe and America after 1917, Berdyaev succeeded in keeping alive the theanthropy that pre-war Englishmen and women found so congenial in Tolstoy and Dostoievsky. For as Berdyaev had said: 'The heroes in Tolstoy's and Dostoievsky's novels were of greater importance for me than philosophical and theological schools of thought, and it was at their hands that I received Christianity' (Berdyaev, 1950, p. 80).

For Berdyaev's own theology was theanthropic, i.e. he held that God and man were inseparable, man being divinely creative like God, or rather co-creative with God. But man's creative calling had yet to be fully realized —this, rather than personal salvation, was man's destiny. Since he could read but little English, Berdyaev feared that the English would not understand what he had to say about Marxism. An Englishwoman—Mrs Florence West—helped him by leaving him the money to buy a house at Clamart in France (Lowrie, 1960, p. 175); and an English publisher, Geoffrey Bles, issued his work in England where it was widely sold and read.

The American Y.M.C.A. virtually kept him alive for most of his years in exile by employing him as editor-in-chief of their publications. They also supported him in his editorship of *Put* (The Way), a critical magazine that he established in 1925 for conducting a high-level dialogue on the present relevance of Christianity. Amongst other participants in this dialogue were Paul Tillich and Jacques Maritain.

In *Put* and at his religious-philosophical academy in Paris from 1924 to 1948, Berdyaev argued that Communism, although marred by crime and violence, nevertheless contained within it undertones of the messianism natural to all religions. Socialism to him was a bourgeois triumph. He argued against abstractions, fictitious economic values and fatalism by bringing Dostoievsky and Tolstoy into the realm of theological discussion. Indeed he has been described as 'the first Christian thinker to take with full seriousness the revolutionary aspect of the Marxist challenge, both in its attack on religious ideologies and its working view of history ... fundamentally revolutionary, more deeply so than Marx, whose impulse in this direction he catches up and develops' (West, 1958, p. 111).

It was ironic that the first effective polemic against planning in Britain—Aldous Huxley's *Brave New World* (1932)—carried as its epigraph a thought of Berdyaev:

> It is possible that a new age is already beginning in which cultured and intelligent people will dream of ways to avoid ideal states and get back to a society that is less 'perfect' and more free.

For Huxley had been a member of a group of English advocates of a national planning policy known as Political and Economic Planning: P.E.P.

P.E.P.

P.E.P. took shape as a result of a disagreement with the proprietor of the *Salisbury Review* over support for Lord Beaverbrook's scheme of Empire free trade. Its founders were Gerald Barry, J. B. Priestley, Ivor Brown, Vernon Bartlett and E. M. Nicholson, who joined together to found the *Week-End Review* in 1930. Its violently critical policy prompted M.P.s to ask what it would do, and as a result Nicholson prepared 'A National Plan for Great Britain'. Published on 14 February 1931 as a sixteen-page supplement the *Review*, it advocated a permanent body to work on planning. It joined up with two discussion groups, one run by Sir Basil Blackett and including Julian Huxley, and another run by Kenneth Lindsay, to form P.E.P. It decided to prepare a national plan by June 1934, working in groups. Meanwhile it issued a broadsheet (*Planning*) that appeared monthly, organized its particular groups, and settled down after 1933 under the chairmanship of I. M. Sieff, of Marks and Spencer. It even weathered Aldous Huxley's send-up of its goals in *Brave New World*.

P.E.P. did not argue alone, for from various salients of intellectuals came sharp reports. The marksman's eye of Barbara (now Lady) Wootton was laid along the sights in her *Plan or No Plan* (1934). This made the point that at least the Russians were trying out new ventures, whereas the West was suffering from 'widespread and disabling paralysis of all collective will' (Wootton, 1934, p. 61). But as far as the Government was concerned, planning was so politically disreputable that, when on 3 April 1935 the prospect was raised in the House of Commons, the debate revealed such prejudice (Hansard 300 No. 72, pp. 377-470) that P.E.P.

devoted a special number (49, 23 April 1935) to countering all the objections advanced against it. As listed there were fourteen: it was against human nature—or British tradition; it meant more centralization and bureaucracy; it stifled individualism among the planned; it demanded supermen as planners; it took away consumers' freedom of choice; it was addictive (i.e. once started it could not be stopped); it led to socialism or Fascism; it bolstered up capitalism; it was international Bolshevism; it led to war; it was an instrument for lowering the status of labour; it was restrictive; and finally, it was a passing fashion.

In citing the two Soviet Five Year Plans (and the British National Budget) as examples of quantitative planning, *Planning* put the case in perspective. But most people probable agreed with the anonymous quotation that Colin Clark used on the title page of his book: 'I think it a disaster for the idea of planning that Russia should have been the country where it has been first tried out' (Clark, 1939).

H. G. Wells

Amongst early investigators of the new Russian Utopia was H. G. Wells. Having written about the future, he went to see to what extent it was working out in Russia. He considered that Lenin, under the stresses of a more pressing reality, was steadily evolving a scheme extraordinarily similar to his own Theory of Revolution by Samurai. Though he was never able to ascertain whether there was any generic connection between the two schemes, he did note that:

> the in-and-out arrangement whereby a man or woman could be a militant member of the organization and then drop out of its obligations and privileges, the imposition

of special disciplines and restrictions upon the active members and the recognition that there are types of good citizens who will live best and work best outside the responsible administrative organization are common alike to any project and the Russian reality. Moreover they resemble each other in insisting upon a training in directive ideas as part of the militant qualifications.

Wells went to see the Foreign Secretary on his return in 1920, and suggested 'a working understanding with the new régime, the giving of technical help of every sort and the exhibition of a manifest care to help'. He argued this would be the best moral and political investment that had ever been offered to Britain. Instead, he found that the British Foreign Secretary regarded Russia as a 'wicked type' of country. He listened to Wells 'as a man listens to a language which he does not understand but which he is quite unwilling to admit is strange to him'. Wells thought that the Foreign Office was 'like a virtuous spinster of a certain age refusing a refusal to elope and bear ten children'. Like Beatrice Webb, Wells called for 'an order of dedicated persons, something resembling the Jesuit order of the Russian Communist Party' (Cole, 1945, p. 148). Wells envisaged his 'open conspiracy' as a group of scientifically trained political commandos, and in *The Open Conspiracy* (1928) outlined the need for a revolutionary élite of high competence, recruited from the science-based professions, to secure immortality of the species through world unity.

The young scientists

Wells's sentiments were echoed by many younger English scientists who, frustrated by the economic depression, felt that there was much to say for obliterating the distinction between 'pure' and 'applied' sciences. Moreover, a steady stream of returning travellers built up, if only incrementally, an impressive picture of the massive organization of science in the Soviet Union. Three were highly articulate: Professor Hyman Levy, Professor J. D. Bernal and Professor J. B. S. Haldane, all lively, provocative, imaginative and capable, exerted themselves in various ways to illuminate the theme—politics. Levy had worked to secure a parliamentary spokesman for science in 1924. His nominee, Major A. G. Church, was the secretary of the three-year-old Association of Scientific Workers. More euphorically, J. B. S. Haldane and J. D. Bernal painted a glittering picture of man's future state, equating this with a régime something on Soviet lines. Of Communism's numerous, able and competent publicists, Bernal was one of the most reputable. He constantly argued that science could no longer stop short at establishing facts, but must go on 'to see that its discoveries are adequately utilized. It was in the Soviet Union that this was first realized' (Bernal, 1939, p. 22). He discounted arguments that this could destroy the spirit which made science possible, and deplored the situation where science would be 'quite a minor and ill-rewarded human occupation, provided that it is left alone by state and industry' (ibid., p. 21).

Other writers with views less intense were Julian Huxley, P. M. S. Blackett and Sir Frederick Gowland Hopkins. But though they did not travel so far along the road to Moscow they shared the commitment of the others to the social functions of Science. This idea was further explored in the imaginative Labour manifesto of G. R. Mitchison in which he argued the necessity of having 'available a very considerable body of intelligent Socialist administrators, both centrally and in the regions, and such persons must have an understanding of the problems with which they are likely to be met' (Mitchison, 1934, p. 9). Subconsciously this technocratic image ignited the imaginations of many British university students. 'Sparked' off (if one may use a Leninist metaphor) in some of the more privileged universities, like Oxford and Cambridge, a consuming flame of enthusiasm (not so much social as technocratic) swept up those in the drab rooms of Redbrick.

The source of the blaze—middle class unemployment—was diagnosed by George Orwell. Describing its manifestation he went on: 'Patriotism, religion, the Empire, the family, the sanctity of marriage, the Old School Tie, birth, breeding, honour, discipline—anyone of ordinary education could turn the whole lot of them inside out in three minutes' (Orwell, 1961, p. 144). The Communist party gave the middle class something to believe in. 'Here was a church, an army, an orthodoxy, a discipline ...The communism of the English intellectual is something explicable enough. It is the patriotism of the deracinated' (ibid., 1961, pp. 144).

S.C.R. and A.Sc.W.

Wells helped promote the Society for Cultural Relations between the Peoples of the British Commonwealth and the U.S.S.R. 'We cannot afford to exist in ignorance of what is going on in Russia in the world of the spirit and Russia cannot afford to go on in isolation', said the *Manchester Guardian* (9 July 1924). The Society's first president was also the first Professor of Sociology at the University of London, L. T. Hobhouse. Another sympathizer was the economist J. M. Keynes who, on his return from Russia, declared that during the next fifty years it would make a larger contribution to the world than any other European country. After 1930 the

Society for Cultural Relations began to organize tours between the two countries. Amongst the first were two tours of thirty and thirty-three scientists, who on their return held a 'we have been to Russia' dinner in October 1931. Educational exhibitions were staged, and schools in Edinburgh, Liverpool, Manchester, Birmingham, London, as well as weekend schools were inaugurated.

Wells's great friend, R. A. Gregory, editor of the leading scientific weekly *Nature* from 1919 onwards, helped publicize his efforts; for Gregory was also the scientific editor of Macmillans, a prestigious moving spirit in the British Science Guild and in the Education Section of the British Association. As such he was able to secure platforms and outlets not only for the educational views of Wells, but of others more directly sympathetic to what Soviet science was trying to accomplish. One such group was the Association of Scientific Workers, formed in 1921 at Cambridge. These views were shared by another liberal publisher, Sir Stanley Unwin, who spoke for many when he deplored Britain's reluctance to leave Russia alone to experiment, 'learning what was to be learnt from it, either positively or negatively'. Like Wells, Sir Stanley deplored our intervention as unjustified and attributed to 'our action in so doing' the 'Soviet suspicions which have dogged our relations ever since' (Unwin, 1960, p. 16).

The C.P.G.B.

The most committed exegetes of Russian planning were, of course, members of the British Communist party, which was known as the Communist Party of Great Britain. As a diasporic agent of Comintern policy, it adopted the resolution of the sixth conference in 1928:

> Being in capitalist society a class economically exploited, politically oppressed, and *culturally choked*, the working class only in the transition period, only *after its conquest of state power*, only by destroying the bourgeois monopoly of education and by mastering all sciences, only in the experience of the greatest constructive work, transforms its own nature (McKenzie, 1964, p. 240).

All schools and universities were by this policy to be captured by the working class following their take-over of power. Printing was to create 'a new socialist culture on a proletarian class base'. All newspapers, books, periodicals, cinemas and theatres were to be state owned. To accelerate the seizure of power, bodies of skilled specialists had to be trained and every emphasis given to the raising of the general cultural level of the proletariat to obliterate class distinctions. Especially did the programme stress the need for a technical intelligentsia (engineers, technicians, organizers, specialists in military affairs). This was to be accompanied by withdrawing state support from religion, and forbidding it to participate in state-supported education. All churches were to be equal, liberty of worship was to be accorded to everyone, whilst 'scientific materialism' was to be promoted by the proletariat.

Many of the expositors of Marxism were far from unintelligent. One of the best, the economist Maurice Dobb, was a particularly astute exponent of the basic importance of mechanization and organization in Russian planning. He was one of the first to show what electrification was doing for the emancipation and elevation of the Russian peasant (Dobb, 1932). For it was the 'red thread' rather than the red threat of Soviet planning that stood out. An English translation of the first Five Year Plan was published by Allen & Unwin in 1930, stressing the triumph of the idea of power development as a basis of economic planning and conservatism. They regarded it as the topical successor to the plan of electrification which Lenin called the second programme of the plan. Two years later Maurice Dobb pointed out 'it was an error to imagine that Soviet Russia pretends to be a Communist system today. She claims to be beginning to be a fully Socialist system: to this the first and second Five Year Plans are only a bridge' (ibid., p. 103). Similarly W. P. and Zelda Coates tabulated the estimated expenditure on education as a science-producing agency during the second Five Year Plan: 22,400 million roubles on general education, 24,100 million on experts and specialists, 4,020 million on advancement of science, 890 million on art, 660 million on the press, 630 million on health and physical training, and 150 million on labour production (Coates, 1934, p. 119).

A rouble was at that time about equivalent to two shillings.

The Russian Communist Party was seen as a new mechanism in society: introducing, explaining and popularizing the social prescriptions of science, it also demanded participation in political activities evoked by those prescriptions. Thus education was, of necessity, Communist, because it was permeated by the spirit of science. As Vova (the Russian archetype) who played in the dialogue of Leonard Barnes in the 1940's the same literary role as Arminius, Baron von Thunder-Ten-Tronckh, did (for Germany) in the dialogue of Matthew Arnold in the 1860s, said: 'As you are fond of putting it, education would be kept in line with communist ideology. We prefer to say that it would be given a scientific foundation. Communism, after all, is simply the application of science to social affairs' (Barnes, 1944, p. 224).

The polytechnic principle

Dr Needham powerfully rebutted the idea that Communism and Christianity were inevitably opposed, or that Communism and Fascism were not. He urged in 1937 that the dichotomy between work and study be abolished and that, as a beginning, Oxford and Cambridge students should be brought closer into contact with the outside world, taking part 'mainly but not necessarily entirely, in their vacation periods, in the actual processes of production'. Since as graduates they would probably be destined for administrative and intellectual positions 'a period, not too short, of genuine manual work side by side with those whose permanent vocation it is, would be of the utmost benefit'. He envisaged some kind of industrial conscription between school and university as 'the army against Nature... to take over some of the more stirring attributes purely military' (Needham, 1946, pp. 105-6). The Soviet 'Rabfacs' also appealed to Needham as 'something like' the type of institution needed for mature students whereby older men and women could enter into the life of the universities in a closer way than they could through the Labour Colleges, the W.E.A. or Extension Classes. 'Perhaps', he added, 'at every university a new college should be built to receive such people' (ibid., p. 111).

Indeed the nucleus of a Communist university was established in an old rectory at Langham, near Colchester, by Middleton Murray, who believed in the necessity of Communism, but denied that its exemplar was Soviet Russia. So did John MacMurray, a particularly influential personality in the Student Christian Movement, for which he wrote *Creative Society: A Study of the Relation of Christianity and Communism* (1935).

A professional engineer-turned-clergyman, the Rev Hewlett Johnson, devoted himself to presenting a slightly more acceptable version of the Russian experiment in corporate living. In this he was helped by his appointment as Dean of Canterbury. Having taken the chair in 1917 for Bertrand Russell at a Welcome-to-Soviet-Russia meeting, he later went on to become the Anglican Church's best known Russophile, the Red Dean. Some think that he was not as effective as the Rev Conrad Noel, the unconventional Vicar of Thaxted in Essex who founded the League of the Kingdom of God and the Catholic Crusade (Groves, 1967). Like Dr Joseph Needham, the biochemist, Noel believed Communism to be the religion of the future, emerging indeed from the ruins of Christianity. Their points of view come through very strongly in *Christianity and the Social Revolution* (1935) and *Christianity and Communism* (1937). All this parallelled what Maurice Hindus observed in Russia where he noticed an 'amazing shift in the ideology of the clergy', many of whom 'propagandize against the sin of personal accumulation and of personal riches'.

> They are for the Kolkhoz. They prove, by holy writ, sometimes with great eloquence, that Christianity was the first to enunciate the sinfulness of the individual accumulation of wealth and the exploitation of labour. The new political ideology of Russian churchmen is a complete reversal from the attitude they had once espoused (Hindus, 1942, p. 237).

Sympathy from 'old India hands'

Shrewdly, the veteran English administrator, Sir John Maynard (who, with Sir Maurice Dwyer, first visited Russia in 1894 and 1895 whilst a Civil Servant in India), emerged from retirement to make two further visits in

1933 and 1935 to assess collective farms. From these he concluded that 'the system of collectivization...did not spring complete and fully armed from the brain of the Communist party' but resulted from 'the Bolshevik method of trial and error applied on an enormous scale'. Sir John Maynard saw the applicability of what the Russians were doing and stood, three times unsuccessfully, as a Labour candidate in order to obtain a platform. Failing this he concentrated on writing *Russia in Flux* (1941) which was described by *The Times* as 'thoughtful, historically sound in essentials and conspicuously fair minded', whilst *The Russian Peasant* (1942) brought into play his vast experience of similar problems in India. Having served as a Vice Chancellor of the University of the Punjab he was uniquely well-qualified to judge the impact of education on the peasantry.

10
Whiffs of realism: 1929-1941

Businessmen and teachers

As the most comprehensive and influential combination of commercial interests that had ever left England, a group of British businessmen (the Anglo-Russian Committee) organized a British Industrial Mission of some eighty-five delegates, which left for Moscow in a special train on 25 March 1929. It was given special treatment in Moscow under the wing of M. Maisky, later to be Russian ambassador to England. On their return one member told the *Manchester Guardian* on 22 April 1929 that 'there are evidences that [the Russians] will put even the United States of America in the shade'. Their report issued on 22 October 1929, was undoubtedly a major factor in securing the renewal of diplomatic relations between the two countries at the end of that year.

A delegation of the Teachers' Labour League also noted that in Russia work was 'the universal shaft around which all instruction and education rotate' (Goode, 1929, p. 20). Curricula were constructed with a view to understanding not only the phenomena of environment, but also man's attempts to control it, and the social effects of such control. Experiments were made in training adults who had missed opportunities under the Tsars; and 'Rabfacs', or workers' faculties of the universities, had been set up. These, incidentally, have contemporary (1968) analogues in England in the Day Release schemes for workers run by the civic universities like Sheffield and Nottingham. This collectivist purpose was epitomized by the Red Army—which the English delegation of the Teachers Labour League described as 'perhaps the most influential of all for adult education' (Goode, 1929, p. 65); by proletcult—the institutional channel for worker's artistic aspirations; and by the Russian development of that great mass medium, the cinema. Indeed, the Russians made the major contribution to the art of the film in the 1920's, a contribution which was not only evinced by *The Battleship Potemkin* or *Ten Days that Shook the World*, but by the mass use of first-class educational films like *The Mechanics of the Brain*. The contrast between the uses made by Russia and England of films in the twenties would be a study in itself.

Films

Films emphasized the symbol of Russian resurgence: the Dneprostroi barrage. Certainly, as it appeared in *Ivan* (one of the many films of the Russian director, Alexander Dovzhenko), it embodied the technocratic maxim that Communism was 'socialism plus electricity'. Other symbols, like the collective farms in *Earth* and the new city in *Frontier*, were invested by Dovzhenko with a significance that made the Russian film a propagandist agency transcending the demands of officialdom.

Film enabled those who could not make the pilgrimage to Russia to have Russia come to them. The revolution lived again in the exciting, glittering documentary of Dziga Vertov who made the Soviet Union's first feature film and issued its first newsreel *Kino Pravda* (*Film Truth*). But Vertov's films were but a prelude to those of V. I. Pudovkin who made films a window through which audiences could see Russia at work (as in the *Mechanics of the Brain* (1926)) or the Russian masses (as in *Storm over Asia* (1928)). However the world at large, rather than the members of avant-garde film societies, identified Russian films with Sergei Eisenstein who, in *The Battleship Potemkin* (1925), so well exploited what he called 'shock attraction' that a historian wrote: 'In no other film has a historic event been reconstructed as a microcosmic symbol of an entire society, nor made so immediate and affecting without an individual hero or personalized story' (Knight, 1959, p. 77).

Bertrand Russell

Though Bertrand Russell felt that 'if a conquering dogmatic Marxism were to replace Christianity, it might be as great an obstacle to progress as Christianity has been' (Russell, 1932, p. 189), he nevertheless greatly admired the Soviet education system because it enabled a child to 'feel, from the first, that he is a unit in Society and has a duty to the community...not so much by precept, but rather by the ordering of his activities'. For this reason he much preferred it to the progressive education of the West where a child was led to grow up either as 'an anarchist, impatient of the restraints of social life', or as an 'isolated unit... frivolous through despair or predatory from agnosticism'. Russell wrote just as the period of experimental education was coming to an end and Bubnov was succeeding Lunacharsky as Commissar. He saw how, in Russia, external hostility produced a war mentality in the schools. After reading the opinions of the President of the Second State University of Moscow, Albert P. Pinkevitch (as outlined in *The New Education in the Soviet Republic* in 1930) he was much impressed by the close similarities with Western institutions and practices. Even the Young Pioneers he found to be 'a copy of the Boy Scouts and [to] have closely similar laws and vows (ibid., 1932, p. 185).

> It is true that the Russian religion, unlike that of Christian countries, is one which most young people who are exposed to it accept enthusiastically and make the basis of their lives. It is true that intelligent people can regard the Russian religion as a means towards the creation of a better world, and can accept its dogmas, at least pragmatically, without intellectual abdication.

But he wondered whether this was only because of its identification with 'a vast half-empty country ripe for development' (ibid., p. 188).

Technology and society

To produce the 'new, proletarian specialists, on whom the Soviet regime could rely wholly and completely in its grand work at the construction of socialism' the central Committee of the Communist Party decreed in 1929 that the Marxist history of technology should be taught. An Institute of the History of Science and Technology was established out of the Commission on the History of Knowledge of the Academy of Sciences, and N. I. Bukhasin put in charge; but after his arrest in 1937 the subject was dropped. However the need to show Russian achievements in this field was emphasized when a new Institute was established in 1945 in the

Academy of Sciences. Technology is to Marxists the crucial element in economic conditions, and after the war became a means of humanizing technical specialists, not only in Russia but in the West too (Joravsky, 1961, pp. 5-6). One of its leading exponents, Professor Zvorikine pointed out that it should broaden the students' outlook, reveal the laws of technical development, and show the triumph of human thought in its fight against the forces of nature' (Zvorikine, 1961, p. 4).

Russian progress (i) technical training

Invited by the Supreme Economic Council to Russia in November 1930 to discuss problems of technical education, Dr B. Mouat Jones of the Manchester College of Technology and J. G. Crowther were embarrassed to find 'that the Soviet had nothing to learn from us, and in fact had interesting lessons to offer' (Crowther, 1932, p. 1). To them, Russian technical education made its English counterpart 'look provincial'. They found no trace of a tendency to give up training in technique for leisure. Especially did they admire the 'monotechnics' for specialisms like turbine engineering and building, each linked to a factory in an organic way and irradiated by the central authority. Another feature which they admired was the training college for teachers of technical subjects, where students were paid wages for studying and participating in the work of the college.

Following their visit, Crowther offered some suggestions as to what we could learn from the Russian example. He would terminate the independence of the local authority, mark down all existing British Technical Colleges as institutions of the second grade and close all technical faculties of universities. In their place he suggested that seven higher technical colleges or technological universities should be established in London, the Midlands, Lancashire, Yorkshire, Wales, the North East Coast, and Scotland. This prescient proposal was to be again put forward, also as a result of Russian example, in 1955, when ten Colleges of Advanced Technology were set up in England and Wales; these were recommended in the Robbins Report of 1963 for upgrading as technological universities. Crowther also recommended the framing of a five year plan for educational development. Especially did he commend the Russian practice of treating all educational and industrial processes as one co-ordinated and indivisible whole.

On his return Dr Mouat Jones, then principal of the Manchester 'Tech', gave eight broadcast talks pointing out that the first Five Year Plan had increased the number of engineers by 250 per cent, reorganized the university course to graduate 12 per cent annually instead of 8 per cent, increased the number of higher technical schools from 14 to 188, and built 663 technicums (or work-based schools). Dr Mouat Jones was, in 1938, to become Vice Chancellor of the University of Leeds and, in 1945, a member of the Percy Committee on Higher Technological Education which recommended the upgrading of the technical colleges and established Regional Advisory Councils for higher education.

Russian progress (ii) a National Health Policy

'The skilfully organized educational party' which Sir Arthur Newsholme identified in 1932 as being directly responsible for the system of socialized medicine in the U.S.S.R. led him to compare its success with British essays in collectivism made during the First World War. He concluded that in Russia the most essential change, as he saw it, was the emancipation of women, which was, 'far reaching and momentous in all grades of society'. Not only did they work beside men in heavy industry, but provided three-quarters of the medical practitioners. Hence the existence of crèches, and the fact that most infants in the U.S.S.R. were born in institutions. With free medical service, not inferior to that in England, centralized clinics and careful co-ordination without parallel in any country in the world, Russia had 'attained at a stride' what was 'only slowly and incompletely being reached in Western countries'. In Britain, he admitted, 'there still exists much awkward dichotomy of public health and clinical medicine, which clogs the wheels of completely satisfactory administration' (ibid., p. 392).

Lord Simon's first warning, 1937

The arrangements for medical care in the schools were described by Lady Simon, an experienced member of the Manchester Education Committee, as 'much more lavish than even in our nursery schools' (Simon, 1937, p. 107), with a permanent nurse and doctor making a daily visit. She was especially impressed by the absence of any selective examination for secondary schools. Children began school at eight and automatically passed to a secondary school at twelve. Instead of a school certificate, there was an internally moderated examination, accompanied by 'a medical examination and a talk with a psychiatrist. The child was then given his results and with it advice about his future, in the presence of a party official'.

Then, and only then, did the pupil opt for one of four courses: (i) to proceed to the eighth class and so to the university (she noted that 55 per cent of Moscow children did this, as opposed to 11·3 per cent of the children in Manchester receiving secondary school allowances based on a means test); (ii) to apply to a technician where, if successful at the entrance examination, he would stay for three or four years. Teachers as well as flour millers were trained in these, but whereas the teachers' technicums were under the Ministry of Education, the others were under the appropriate commissariat; (iii) to attend a factory school for two years and be trained as a skilled worker in vocational subjects, working for an examination called the 'technical minimum'; (iv) to go directly into industry working part time until he is eighteen. Here, too, he could take the 'technical minimum'. Such a programme, of course, involved a high-degree of use of school holidays, and two—even three—shift systems were employed. Lenin's maxim, that 'without books there can be no knowledge, without knowledge there can be no communism', seemed to Lady Simon to explain the strict subordination of the individual to the pre-determined end; she deplored the lack of individual, local and professional freedom so evident in England. The enormous drive that swept all these freedoms away impressed her but she doubted whether it was, in any relevant sense of the term, education.

The Simons had been stimulated by the Webbs to investigate the local government of Moscow, the Mossoviet. Sir Ernest (later Lord) Simon concluded that though there was 'much in the powerful drive and leadership of their one-party system and in some aspects of their socialism that we must wholeheartedly admire and from which we must endeavour to learn', he could not conceive of 'any British democrat who, in order to obtain these undoubted advantages, would be willing for one moment to consider abandoning our traditional methods of freedom, of toleration, of kindliness, and of consideration for the rights of every individual'. He asked if the English could 'achieve something of the leadership and enthusiasm of Moscow while maintaining the freedom of minorities and the kindly tolerance of England?' and concluded: 'That is the problem on the solution of which the future of British democracy depends' (ibid., pp. 193, 227).

The Left Book Club

That problem was collectively analysed and debated in one of the most remarkable secular conventicles of the thirties. The Left Book Club. Its 'onlie begetter' was that enterprizing publisher, Mr Victor Gollancz, who, in 1935, suggested to one of his Marxist authors, John Strachey, that a Left Book Club should be established to provide readers with cheap and regular pastoral information on Socialism—and on its critics. He then appointed the Rev John Lewis, a non-conformist clergyman, to organize local discussion groups around the 'selected books'. The selectors were Gollancz, Strachey and Laski. This new Trinity relieved the 'faithful' of the necessity of choosing books for themselves. As a bookseller wrote:

> We don't have to hum and ha,
> Nous avons changé tout cela—
> Our books are chosen for us—thanks
> To Strachey, Laski and Gollancz (Samuels, 1966, p. 65).

As members thumbed the monthly orange-backed book, any hesitations about their purchase were overcome when they read the *Left Book News*, which told them all about the selection. After May 1936, at their heels and organizing them into discussion groups, was the Rev John Lewis. Groups had representatives at regional conferences; regional conferences led to annual con-

THE RUSSIAN INFLUENCE ON ENGLISH EDUCATION

ferences. A *Handbook for Local Groups* was issued and, where this failed, travelling organizers came down to visit.

No evangel, not that of Rev Frank Buchman, had such an immediate, if ephemeral, success. From 6,000 in the first month, membership rose to 40,000 by the end of the year, and to 57,000 by 1939. Nor were members content to hold discussion groups only, for they acquired coffee bars, libraries, classrooms and halls. By 1939 there were 1,200 groups, actively undertaking, under the tutelage of the three wise men of Henrietta Street, intensive group therapy of 'conversion' to true socialism. That the ideal was Russia can be seen from the fact that the Communist Party publishers, Lawrence and Wishart, also offered their books at reduced prices to members, some of whom even joined the party. Rightly is the Club given some credit for the increase of Communist Party membership from 6,500 in 1935 to 16,000 in 1938. For as 'the greatest single force in England for the dissemination of left wing thought' it 'injected, especially through the works of Strachey, the first effective dose of Marxism into the English cultural blood stream' (ibid., p. 84). The atmosphere of a Left Book Club meeting was caught by George Orwell in *Coming Up for Air*. Elsewhere, in *Inside the Whale and other Essays*, he described 'the central stream of English literature' as being, for three years, 'more or less under Communist control'. Orwell took part with 2,762 other British volunteers in the Spanish Civil War.

The Webbs' report

Perhaps the greatest achievement of the Left Book Club was to remove the question mark from the title of the 1,000-page report on the Soviet Union by its veteran

English assessors, Sidney and Beatrice Webb: *Soviet Communism: A New Civilization?* (1935). The Webbs showed that Soviet Russia was executing, on a larger scale, ideas first propounded by the nineteenth-century British manufacturer, Robert Owen. In so doing, it had unleashed 'enormous energy' by 'its drastic ousting of all disqualifications of sex or race, inferiority of social position or lack of means' (Webb, 1935, p. 102). The Webbs adopted a stance which would have done credit to Bazarov:

> It seems as if the British conception of culture were closely bound up with the absence of any use-value in the pursuit or practice of the cultured life, apart from what may be admitted to be the utility of promoting culture itself. In Britain the devotee of culture is apt to regard, with what the soviet communists think a silly complacency, the fact that his efforts to increase or develop his own culture are divorced from any practical use in the transformation of the world (ibid., 1935, p. 923).

Contrasting Soviet 'polytechnicalization' of all education from the school to the university, the Webbs held up the 'regrettable dichotomy' of British education and social organization, where:

> Scientists and technologists, whose work is changing the material basis of civilization, are too often trained in complete ignorance of the social results of their activities and of the social responsibilities these entail; whilst statesmen, historians and sociologists are generally educated in ignorance of the technological changes which do so much to mould the character of our civilization (ibid., 1935, p. 955).

Stressing the 'dialectical implications of science', they suggested that: 'these aspects of science are not always borne in mind in the scientist's own studies, when he shuts himself up in his own narrow specialism, which he may even delight in keeping what he calls 'pure' and unconnected with the world of action'.

In 1941 the Russians were withstanding the fury of a German invasion that had looked only too likely to be directed against England. So, when the Webb's massive endorsement of Soviet organization appeared, Englishmen were less inhibited about reading accounts of a country which, by diverting the German panzers, had now become a gallant ally.

11
The Second World War and after: 1941-1957

Communism and managerialism

A new image of the Russians as the nation which had 'advanced farthest along the managerial road' was presented by James Burnham's *Managerial Revolution* (1941). It harmonized with the need to plan for victory. New ministries, like that of Aircraft Production, were also propelling Britain along a fast road where speed was maintained by norms (Burnham, 1962, pp. 201, 236). Indeed war administrators, like George Dickson, could be found to argue that wartime Regional Production organizations should be adapted for peacetime planning. Russia's dramatic resistance to the German military machine, which might otherwise have been directed against England, further tempered the outlook. Herbert Morrison, the Home Secretary, went on record as saying that 'in applying the principles of public ownership and management to the extent it considers to be practicable, the Soviet Government is conducting the greatest economic experiment of our time' (Morrison, 1944, p. 5). This comment was made during a Fabian symposium.

Experience in England's collectivized wartime economy strengthened the feeling that perhaps public ownership of the means of production would be more desirable at the end of the war than the pre-war anarchy. The distinguished historian E. H. Carr hit the right note with his observation that:

> the impact of the Soviet Union has fallen on a Western World where much of the framework of individualism was already in decay, where faith in the self-sufficiency of individual reason had been sapped by the critique of relativism, where the democratic community was in urgent need of reinforcement against the forces of disintegration inherent in individualism, and where the technical conditions of production on the one hand and the social pressures of mass civilization on the other, were already imposing far-reaching measures of collective organization (Carr, 1946, p. 116).

'Even to reach full employment', Thomas Balogh had argued, the Government should possess means of control which hitherto had been denounced by the 'liberals' and the U.S.A. (Bernal, 1944, p. 123). For although Russia had been far more weakened by the war than the Western powers, her economic system 'made possible efforts of a scale which in individualist societies would be impossible' (ibid., p. 134).

Pressure for the comprehensive school

In exerting pressure to secure the framing of an equitable Education Act of 1944, the Campaign for Educational Advance was itself pressured by the Communist Party of Great Britain to press for 'a new type of secondary school' which would 'avoid the inadequacies and inequalities of present-day secondary education'; to 'fully integrate Public and Private Schools into a unified state system and provide a common form of education for all children up to sixteen years of age'. This would necessitate abandoning selection at eleven or thirteen, a process described as 'educationally unsound' since 'teachers cannot determine their pupils' ability and interests when they are so young, nor should the children bear the responsibility of deciding their future.' The C.P.G.B. argued from Russian practice where it was necessary to direct resources towards teaching rather than testing, and where intelligence tests had been abolished on 4 July 1936 because they tended to mandarinize society and foster a negativism in the 'rejected': the decree of abolition was entitled 'On Pedological Perversions in the System of the Peoples' Commissariat of Education'.

The effect of this abolition in Russia was startling. An American psychologist described the 'almost complete disappearance of all work connected with psychotechnics and the testing movement' as 'striking' (Bauer, 1952, p. 160). The realization that the long haul to reconstruction would involve giving the 'creative capacities of the workers a central purpose which it had not had since the break-up of the Middle Ages' (the words were those of Henry F. Ward on the Soviet Union but the spirit was that of Aneurin Bevan), probably led to the election of a Labour Government in 1945. And in its first flush of power, this government acknowledged its debts, notably in the official foreword to the centenary edition of the *Communist Manifesto*. In it, Harold Laski paid tribute to the 'common inspiration' that led the Labour Party to have 'largely established free education for all children in publicly-owned schools' (Laski, 1948, p. 7).

The debate about the crisis in universities

Second to the U.S.A. in the number of universities (690 as opposed to 716), and second in the degree of financial support accorded to universities (90 million as opposed to 100 million), the U.S.S.R. was nevertheless far ahead of Britain (which had only sixty such institutions enjoying some 6½ million of income). Even Germany with 115 institutions enjoying 28½ million was superior (Hutton, 1943). So it is not surprising that the C.P.G.B. called for university status to be accorded to English technical colleges. These were also to give a free training with maintenance grants in order to tap 'our great reservoirs of technical ability' (Communist Party, 1943, pp. 29-30). As we have seen, (*ante* p. 92) the Percy Committee on Higher Technological Education flirted with the idea; out of its report emerged a series of regional councils on higher education, all consultative bodies.

So strongly vocal were the protagonists of the idea that English universities should be centrally planned (to ensure that studies were related to social welfare and practical needs), that a group was formed to combat this. Indeed, of the many groups trying to conserve 'freedom' in science and education, this was perhaps the most effective, since its spokesman was the chairman of the University Grants Committee. In his *Crisis in the University* (1948) he admitted that though the traditional Christian concept had little relevance to present conditions, there was need of a common ideal for the universities that was non-Marxist. Marxist ideas, he argued, would reduce universities to the status of state churches. But when he criticized the existing system for not stimulating students to ask 'fundamental questions' he was virtually inciting them to apply the only criterion they knew, i.e. utility. 'Utility' found powerful support from non-Marxists, who were quite prepared to assess Russia on her achievement rather than aspiration. 'There is no doubt that the masses are becoming science-conscious in a way not known before in Russia, or indeed, anywhere in the world', wrote the Australian scientific attaché in Russia (Ashby, 1947, pp. 196-7). There the 'brightest minds' (ibid., p. 192), who usually could read French, German and English 'with ease' (ibid., p. 202), and who were collectively 'Britain's keenest ally in our efforts to break down government-imposed barriers and remove government-inspired suspicion in the Soviet Union', were scientists. (ibid., p. 202). They were also 'the only large group of Russians who are obliged by their profession to remain constantly in touch with British thought' (ibid., p. 206).

Unfortunately, at this moment, British thought was polarized against such contact by the Lysenko affair. Lysenko was claiming to have done for wheat what his educational counterparts were hoping to do for children. This led to another scientist, erstwhile well-disposed (Sir Julian Huxley), to describe the Soviet Union as having repudiated 'certain basic elements of scientific method', and by so doing, repudiating 'the universal and supranatural character of science'. (in *Nature*, 163, 1949). The Lysenko affair was followed by the imposition of a virtual censorship by the U.S.A. on pro-Russian books, culminating in the 'witch hunt' mounted by Senator MacCarthy. Confusion of purpose over Germany led the U.S.A. to adopt a posture of unconditional hostility to the U.S.S.R. As one of America's pensioners Britain also adopted this attitude, since the golden passage across the Atlantic might be, and often was, barred to teachers if they incautiously, by word or deed, seemed to endorse anything good in the U.S.S.R.

Lord Simon's second warning, 1956

Yet the United States, in the person of Dr N. de Witt, led the British government to admit that, with only fifty-seven engineers per million of the population graduating annually, it was falling behind West Germany (86), France (70), the U.S.A. (136) and, above all, the U.S.S.R. (286). (That this official admission on the part of the government was based on the calculations of an American was even further evidence of our dependency). 'Close equivalence, and occasionally...numerical superiority' was his verdict on the Soviet as compared to American production of specialists in science, engineering, medicine and agriculture (de Witt, 1955, p. 256). Objectively quantitative, he followed the flow of students through the various channels of the Soviet system from the primary school to the most advanced doctoral degree, and endorsed flexibility in the upper levels.

Unlike England (which virtually adopted the idea of the university-based Ph. D. from the U.S.A., after the First World War), the U.S.S.R. organized its advanced degrees both in the universities and research institutes. Nor did it allow these degrees to be awarded by universities, but by a body transcending these—the Supreme Attestation Commission (U.A.K.). Established in 1938, this not only granted and confirmed such degrees but also ratified academic and research appointments. Before and after its establishment, the necessary steps for establishing two advanced academic degrees were taken —the aspirantura training leading to the candidate degree and the docturantura training leading to a doctor's degree. Amongst the fields recognized for such training are pedagogy and, at the aspirantura level, physical education. Helped by the all-party Parliamentary and Scientific Committee, which could appreciate Russian achievement divorced from any ideological commitment, the moral of all this seeped slowly into the consciousness of English politicians of every political colour. This probably accounted for the fact that, with regard to industrial research, a similar programme was set up in England in 1956 when the National Council for Technological Awards (established in that year) made provision for granting Masters' and Doctors' degrees for work in industry.

Evidence of Russian achievement was impressively deployed in the House of Lords on 21 November 1956 by Lord Simon of Wythenshawe, the industrial chairman of the Council of Manchester University and founder of the *Universities Quarterly*. Describing himself as 'very frightened of the position into which England had been manoeuvred by short-sighted educational policies', he cited the opinions of numerous English missions to Russia, especially that of the steel industry mission which found that Russian output would increase, by 1960, from twice to three times the size of our own. Since the output of Russian scientists and engineers was increasing by 10 per cent each year, he called for a 'crash programme' to tip the scales in favour of Britain. Supporting him, Lord Chorley (secretary of the Association of University Teachers) forecast the impressiveness of Russian competition. But their ideas, argued the Marquis of Salisbury, would, if implemented, do serious harm to the economy as a whole; while Lord Halsbury, Chairman of the National Research and Development Corporation, protested against the foolishness of making Russian progress the reason for the further development of English higher education.

Russia in Europe

By 1943 the veteran English geographer, Sir Holford Mackinder, had reached the 'unavoidable conclusion' that 'if the Soviet Union emerges from this war as conqueror of Germany, she must rank as the greatest land power on the globe. Moreover, she will be a power in the strategically strongest defensive position. The Heartland is the greatest natural fortress on earth. For the first time in history it is manned by a garrison sufficient both in number and quality' (Mackinder, 1943). Such an opinion tapped fears deep in English historical consciousness. The sheer size of Russia had affected one Englishman two centuries earlier. 'I cannot avoid beholding the Russian empire as the native enemy of the north-western parts of Europe', wrote Oliver Goldsmith in the *Public Ledger* on 31 October 1760, 'an enemy already possessed of great strength and, from the nature of the government, every day threatening to become more powerful' (Friedman, 1966, p. 353). A century later. Marx frightened readers of the *New York Tribune* (1 June 1853) with his statement that: 'Since Peter the Great the Russian frontier had advanced.

Towards Berlin, Dresden and Vienna about 700 miles
Towards Constantinople 500 miles
Towards Stockholm 630 miles
Towards Teheran 1000 miles

The war left Russia controlling half Europe. The preservation of the other half was in the hands of the Americans. The second half decided rapidly (the Schumann declaration) to unite their Coal and Steel Resources in a Community (E.C.S.C.) which was established in 1951, and their atomic energy in another (EURATOM) established in 1958. In the intervening seven years other proposals for uniting agriculture, health and transport were made; but the landmark was the signature of the Treaty of Rome in 1957 which provided further impetus for integration by establishing the Common Market—a free trade area in tariff, labour and capital. But 1957 was notable for another evidence of Russian technological superiority: the launching of 'sputnik'. This precipitated yet further changes, as will be shown in the next chapter.

12
The post-sputnik era: 1957-1969

The galvanizing of the U.S.A.

The first sputnik ascended and orbited on 4 October 1957. A second (nearly five times as heavy) went into orbit a month later, and a third (fifteen times as heavy) on 15 May 1958. By 2 January 1959 the Russians had launched, in the direction of the moon, a cosmic rocket which went into orbit as a satellite of the solar system. These sputniks highlighted Russian computational and engineering skill and the reservoir of scientific talent on which it could now draw. Sputniks so alarmed Americans that their president complained that they began to demand 'vastly increased spending so as to turn nearly every student into a scientist or engineer as quickly as possible' (Eisenhower, 1966, p. 241). The president himself appointed a Special Assistant for Science and Technology, and established a Science Advisory Committee, whilst a National Defence Education Act was passed on 2 September 1958 giving grants for improving school instruction in science, mathematics and modern languages, for training school counsellors, for fellowships, for college teachers and for student loans.

All this had reverberated back in Britain where Harold Macmillan had risen to the premiership. Twenty years earlier he had, with Allan Young, an ex-Marxist from the Clyde, formed 'The Next Five Years Group' to promote the establishment of a central planning staff, the nationalization of public utilities and the Bank of England, and the raising of the school-leaving age. To sow the seeds of these ideas Macmillan and Young established a newspaper called *The New Outlook*, and issued cogently argued manifestos such as *The Next Five Years* (1935) and *The Middle Way* (1938). Indeed Macmillan became so identified with the case for nationalization that he confessed to his constituents in 1939 that he was looked on as 'a bit of a Bolshie' (Sampson, 1967, pp. 31-52). Twenty years later, in 1959, he established a Ministry of Science and in 1962 a National Economic Development Council. Since the United States was the country with which Mr Macmillan claimed a 'special relationship', he noted the massive federal action taken to improve the productivity of their educational system. So the American National Defence Education Act in turn stimulated English activity in these fields, in particular the Nuffield projects currently (1968) being mounted. So, too, successive English attempts first, to form one, then, to join another grouping of European powers were motivated by the need to avoid being swamped by large-scale Russian (or indeed American) enterprises.

Lord Simon's third warning, 1960

Meanwhile in England Lord Simon asked, on 11 May 1960, for the appointment of a Committee to inquire and report on the extent and nature of the provision of full-time education for those over the age of eighteen, whether in universities or elsewhere. He pointed out that, having doubled over the last twenty years to 100,000, the number of university students was likely to double again in the next twenty, and significantly asked 'whether we were learning what we can from foreign universities... since the wide organization of M.I.T., of Cal. Tech., of various Russian universities and of Aachen and Zurich is in many ways in advance of what we have done here' (Hansard, 11 May 1960).

The matter, as Lord Hailsham agreed (ibid., pp. 621, 726), was too urgent for the cumbersome machinery of a Royal Commission; but he asked for permission to reflect on it. That reflection lasted for seven months till, on 20 December 1961, Mr Macmillan announced the appointment of a prime minister's committee under Lord Robbins to undertake not only what Lord Simon had suggested, but also to advise H.M. Government of the principles upon which the long-term development of higher education should be based. Not surprisingly, in view of its origin, the Robbins Committee visited Russia. They found that the growth of higher education there was 'quite extraordinary', rising from 130,000 students in 1917 to nearly 2,400,000 in 1960, with the result that its output of scientists and technologists was 'considerably greater' than that of the United States. By comparison Britain's discrepancies were described as 'striking' (H.M.S.O., Cmnd. 2154-V, 1963, p. 189). The Prime Minister's Committee selected five features of the Soviet system for special comment. Most important was its use of education 'both as an instrument of social policy and to manipulate the supply of trained manpower in a deliberate and detailed manner'; a striking contrast to the Western way of thinking. Second, the complete professionalization of higher education which enabled the holder of every qualification to practice his or her profession. Third, the meagre (24 per cent) proportion of women students in higher education in Britain compared with that in Russia (45 per cent). Fourth, the over-riding concern for the social integration of the intelligentsia and the working population which led to 'practical work and manual labour being required of all pupils and students in varying degrees from the age of twelve upwards'. Last, the 'heavy reliance' placed upon part-time study in the evenings and (even more) upon correspondence courses; they noted that the proportional effort devoted to the latter was to increase. All five points were to become part of the recommendations of the Robbins Committee. As a result of them, and of the recommendations of another working party—The Trend Committee—which reported at the same time, the five-year-old Ministry of Science was merged with the Ministry of Education into the Department of Education and Science on 1 April 1964.

Other developments, like the University of the Air, the establishment of the Council of Academic Awards and the polytechnics, no less than the acceptance of the principle of forward planning, showed that foreign examples in the U.S.A. and the U.S.S.R. have not been forgotten.

Sir Leon Bagrit and day boarding schools

Called upon to deliver the Reith Lectures in 1964, Sir Leon Bagrit cited the rapid progress of Russian industry under the stimulus of automation. Its basis, he pointed out, was an educational programme in 1948 directed to launching the Automation Seven Year Plan in 1959. He warned that if Britain failed 'to promote automation energetically here, we shall find ourselves eventually facing not only massive American competition but

Russian competition too' (Bagrit, 1965, p. 52). Bagrit was, aptly enough, the son of a Russian emigré. He suggested 'day boarding schools' where boys of particular promise could go at breakfast and stay till the evening. In this longer school day 'it should be easier to instil in them the type of attitudes which are necessary if we are going to develop the social conscience and sense of social responsibility which an age of plenty is going to demand' (ibid., p. 37). By this suggestion Bagrit, involuntarily perhaps, drew popular attention to the *internats*, or Russian boarding schools. They had been described by the *Times Educational Supplement* as early as 24 February 1956, and an account of *Internat No. 10* in Moscow had been given to readers of *The Times* on 18 January 1960. A means of preparation for a collective society, its curriculum was that of a progressive boarding school in war time, with early rising, exercise, involvement in a 'useful' project and pioneer meetings (a cross between the Scouts and an O.T.C.). Khruschev put the case for their establishment before the Central Committee of the Communist Party:

> In the recent past, the ruling classes used a way other than the general school to bring up the younger generation in accordance with principles reflecting the existing social order and its prevailing spirit. The government formed special schools of learning, for children, such as page and cadet schools, and girls' schools. In these boarding schools, the children of the ruling class received their aristocratic education (Redl, 1964, p. 181).

He was also frank about the reasons for establishing them:

> As a result of the war, our many widows have the complicated task of bringing up children by themselves. Also, many of our families, where both parents work can only devote themselves to educating their children on a

part-time basis. As a result, many children are left in the care of other people, neighbours or relatives, or often left without adequate adult supervision, which frequently leads to sad consequences (Redl, 1964, p. 180).

The first internats opened were those from grades 1 to 5 (ages seven to fourteen). Ranging in size from 200 to 600 boarders, they had an additional complement (not exceeding one third) of day boys. They began in schools, pedagogical institutes or children's homes, and had farms attached. Apart from the teachers there was a special group, known as 'upbringers', who acted as moral tutors. English readers of the *Times Educational Supplement* were told on 2 March 1962 that, within five years, 1990 such internats had been established with a total population of half-a-million pupils. It was calculated that the number of pupils would quintuple under the 1959-1965 Seven Year Plan. As two Soviet educationists (E. I. Afanasenko and I. A. Kairov) wrote:

> For the first time in the history of the Soviet educational system, there are institutions of learning which encompass widely diversified age groups under one roof. These school internats provide the youngster with learning experiences from the time he is one year old to the period of completing secondary schooling and choosing a profession at seventeen years of age (Redl, 1964, p. 200).

With their own journal *School Internat*, a laboratory school and a policy of avoiding the creation of élitist or 'backwood' *internats*, these schools made a great impression on English-speaking countries.

The spirit of Makarenko

When an American asked the director of one of the Moscow boarding schools 'if he had taken Makarenko as his model' he answered with a qualified 'yes'. 'Here,' continued the American, 'as in other schools I visited, it was pointed out that Makarenko worked under conditions rather different from those prevailing in Soviet schools today. Although the directors spoke of him with admiration, they are seeking to capture the spirit of his achievements without copying him literally.' Certainly the Americans thought that these boarding schools were 'far from being Soviet Etons and Harrows, as the foreign press suggested' (Lilge, 1958, p. 50).

Makarenko was the Soviet Union's major educational experimenter. Within the two years after the First World War he had transformed the Gorki Colony (near Poltava) from a centre for orphans into a showplace for the reclamation of the 'morally defective'. When it moved to Trepke, he developed the system of 'detachments' which Lucy L. Wilson thought were more democratic than those of the George Junior Republic. When it moved to the disused monastery of Kuriajh (near Kharkov), Makarenko imposed a quasi-military sense of duty on his charges. In 1927, he was given yet another colony of delinquents at Kharkov, called after F. E. Dzerjhinski, a stalwart of the secret police, and in running this colony from 1928 to 1935 perfected the idea of training delinquents by creating a soviet of its inmates. He used English public school concepts like duty, honour, purposefulness, courage and discipline as developed by labour tasks, to strike responsive chords in the delinquents. His practice of four hours work and four hours school in the Dzerjhinski Commune was highly successful. His students not only worked on farms but also built and operated, for the first time in Russia, such complex apparatus as cameras and electric drills (Medynsky, 1943, pp. 32-3).

War brought appreciation of Makarenko's 'essential

principle': 'always to demand as much as possible from a man, but at the same time show him as much respect as possible,... we cannot demand much of a person whom we do not respect' (ibid., p. 33). After his death and the Second World War, Makarenko's ideas acquired added relevance. Karl Mannheim saw how the group loyalty cultivated in English public schools was analogous to that inculcated by collective farms in Russia. One produced keen athletically-minded administrators: the other transformed the slow backward peasant of Tsarist days into the eager, technically-minded collective farmer of Soviet Russia (ibid., p. 75). A similar comparison was made by John Pringle in *Encounter* (February 1961). By the 1950s accounts of his works began to filter slowly through the linguistic barrier. Apart from Gorki's enthusiastic references and Lucy Wilson's notice (1928) it was not until Medynsky (1943), Goodman (1949), and the translations of the Litvinovs and Stephen Garry, that English readers were provided with a fuller picture of the man who came to be regarded as the Soviet Union's best-known educational theorist.

The influence of Strumilin

As the accent on school as opposed to home intensified, the well-known Soviet economist S. G. Strumilin wrote:

> A group of normal children, in particular if it is guided by an experienced teacher, can give a child much more than the most loving mother. The unanimous reaction of such a group to any anti-social inclinations on the part of the child will nip these in the bud. At the same time, all his natural social instincts and sympathies will develop in the collective, in the process of intercourse with other children, and will be strengthened by the daily work of the Soviet School and preschools establishment.

He forecast that in fifteen or twenty years time, 'every Soviet family, if it so wishes, will be able to keep a child at a nursery, a kindergarten with 24-hour maintenance, and later at a boarding school. All these establishments will be maintained by the State' (Strumilin, 1964, pp. 95-6).

Forecasting, from strictly utilitarian premises, has been Strumilin's occupation for nearly half a century. He was and is a leading proponent of Soviet planning in the top echelons of GOSPLAN, of which he became deputy chairman. Also, as chief of the Central Statistical Administration he has evolved criteria of priorities which, as education became an integral factor in national planning, has influenced English thought on this subject. Himself a graduate of the St Petersburg polytechnic, with experience of heavy work on a building site and of teaching factory workers, he has a most realistic approach to planning for a system of targets rather than forecasting general trends as some others did. His impact on Russian plans was so considerable (Davies, 1960, pp. 286-296) that, as British, French and other economists moved into his field, they inevitably had to reckon with him. Certainly his calculations of the profitability of educational investment and the returns from it, especially in the productivity of labour as outlined in the UNESCO publication: *International Social Science Bulletin* in 1962 (Vol. 14, No. 4, pp. 633-636) were a landmark. And from that time on, the issue of central investment planning (as in Russia) versus indicative 'planning' (as in France and Britain) has become such an increasingly important component of educational theory: so much so that the *Yearbook of Education* devoted its 1967 edition to a comprehensive survey of it. It is therefore not without interest to note that, by 1985, it is envisaged that the number of these who will have completed higher education in Russia will have increased by a factor of 2·3, to 15 millions, whilst those with secondary education will have also increased by a similar factor (Goodman and Feshbach, 1967, p.i.). Moreover the percentage of those completing higher education is expected to rise from 1·3 per cent in 1950 to 6·5 per cent in 1985; those completing specialized secondary education to rise from 3·4 per cent in 1950 to nearly 11 per cent in 1985, and those completing a general secondary education to rise from 4·3 per cent to 11·8 per cent over the same period.

The 1958 and 1964 reforms

Strumilin's estimate that 23 per cent of the national income in 1960 resulted from increased skills obtained through education was cited by a special mission of the International Institute of Educational Planning. For in Russia special schools for mathematical talent existed side by side with comprehensive education up to the age of fifteen, with a polytechnic topping. Here the 1958 reforms were especially relevant. They were inaugurated by Khruschev's speech in that year to the thirteenth congress of the Komsomol, reproaching them for their attitude to work in factories and farms. He warned them that four-fifths of the available places at the universities would be reserved for those who had already spent two years in practical work. This meant that the last two years of the ten years of formal education was lopped off, and that college-bound students had to study in their spare time by correspondence or evening work.

The underlying aim of the 1958 reforms appears to have been to reverse the Stalinist trend towards an academic education in a ten-year (occasionally eleven-year ultimately twelve-year) school, and to turn Soviet education back into a Leninist direction with education seen both as a preparation for and a part of life (=work). The main opponents of the reforms seem to have been among the academics in the ten-year (eleven-year) schools and the universities, the neo-bourgeois parents, and the young people leaving the ten-year (eleven-year) schools at seventeen or eighteen. Criticism of the quality of the polytechnical element in higher courses, of the two-year work requirement before University, of string-pulling by influential parents, and of conditions in shift schools and institutes, have been made public in the U.S.S.R.; and the 1964 reform of the secondary schools could be seen both as a further attempt to clip the wings of the academics by a reduction of the 'sixth-form' course from three to two years, and as an admission of the ineffectiveness of the polytechnical element in the course in that the percentage of time in each year devoted to this has been reduced. The reservation of 20 per cent of University places for gifted scientists to proceed directly from school to university (and the re-introduction of specialization into the school-leaving examination in 1964) can be seen as a victory for the academics.

Anglo-Russian co-operation

Realization of the mutual advantages to be obtained by co-operation led industrial leaders in the United Kingdom (represented by the Confederation of British Industry) and the U.S.S.R. (represented by the Soviet State Committee for Science and Technology) to conclude an agreement. The first steps were taken in September 1967 when Sir Stephen Brown led a team of captains of British industry to Russia. An agreement was signed between the two countries whereby eight joint working groups were set up to explore possibilities in the fields of power, engineering, metallurgy, industrial pollution, patents, rail transport, standards, and scientific instruments. Their work was reviewed in May 1968 and five more groups were established, this time to study machine tools, building construction, coalmining, food and food machinery, and information storage and retrieval.

As the chairman of the Confederation of British Industry said: 'We believe that the gap can be bridged. Given patience and time, there is no reason why technological co-operation between a socialist and a mixed economy should not become big business' (Davies, 1968, p.v.). Noting that this agreement for Co-operation in Applied Science and Technology was both a significant example of co-operation between the Soviet Union and the rest of Europe and part of a major drive to sell patents, licences, plant and machinery abroad, two Englishmen commented: 'if the Soviet drive to improve the rate of technical innovation is successful, the Soviet technological advance in some major industries could present a serious economic challenge to other industrialized countries' (Davies and Berry, 1968, p. 131).

13
Conclusion

The dead-end of all discussion

'You can always stump them with Russia; they can always stump each other... Its the dead end of all discussion'. So Ambrose in Evelyn Waugh's *Put Out More Flags* (1942).

Suspicion of Russophiles goes back a long time. Two hundred and seventy years ago the author of the first Russian grammar to be published in England was described as 'addicted to reading the books of the Rosy-Crucians & Millenaryes, whose tenents prevayled so far upon his deluded Phansy and judgment, that he has printed some things in defense of those Whimsyes and fooleryes' (Simmons, 1950, p. 105). This suspicion is also the built-in probability co-efficient which Russian writers have taken for granted for a century and more, ever since Couerderoy conjured up the spectacle of revolutionary Cossacks overturning state, religion and private property (1854), and his friend Hedder argued that the communal system of land tenure in Russia 'answers better to the ideal dreamed of by Europe than the way of life of the Graeco-Roman world' (Carr, 1952, p. 83). Now events move so rapidly that even tolerant Westerners

CONCLUSION

have to change their ground. Toynbee thought that through increasing mechanization Russia would gradually cease to denounce 'Western values', but after the war he was discounting both 'dogmatic optimism' and 'dogmatic pessimism' and counselling mankind 'to reconcile itself as best it could to the disturbing knowledge that it was facing issues in which its very existence might be at stake, and that it was at the same time impossible at this stage to guess what the event would be' (Toynbee, 1939-61, ix, p. 535). This change of outlook was sometimes more startling, as in the case of some millenarians who loudly complained that the light they had detected in the East had been switched off. In addition to those testifying to Mr Crossman's book, *The God that Failed*, 1950, individual complaints were made by John T. Murphy (1941), Freda Utley (1949), Douglas Hyde (1951), Philip Toynbee (1954) and Claude Cockburn (1956, 1958).

Yet another cause of misunderstanding is the stripping of English imperial trappings as the Russians don theirs. Not even Professor Toynbee's attempts to discover a syncretic religion arising out of this conflict of East and West seems to have improved matters. Then again, there have been a series of alarms concerned with Russian spying: Alan Nunn May, Pontecorvo, the defections of Burgess and McLean, and later of Philby. Indeed the Radcliffe Committee in 1962 expressed its disturbance 'at the number of Communist sympathizers holding positions as paid officials or unpaid officers in Civil Service staff associations and trade unions'.

The real iron curtain

But the real iron curtain has been one of language. In spite of the suggestion made at the beginning of this century that Russian should replace Latin as a school subject (*Spectator*, 22 November 1902) progress has been slow. By warning against 'undue precipitation' in developing the study of Russia in the (then) fifteen universities of Great Britain, a committee set up in 1916 by the Prime Minister to study the promotion of modern languages as subjects of study described Russia's history as 'amorphous, obscure, unaccented and uninspiring' and its literature as seeming 'to have little educational value' (H.M.S.O. Cd. 9036, 1918, p.64). This was in spite of their recognition that relations with Russia could only be opened 'by a nation which has studied, as well as the language of Russia, her social anatomy, the character of her people, her geography, and her economic conditions and capacities'. They placed it, with Spanish, last on the preference list, behind French, German and Italian. Such 'undue precipitation' was certainly avoided. For not until the Norwood Committee came out in 1943 with a strong recommendation in their favour were intensive two-year courses given to sixth formers. Even these grew so slowly (in spite of Modern Languages *Pamphlet* No. 29, and the efforts of the Joint Services Course for Linguists) that the Annan Committee found, in 1962, only one candidate offering Russian at 'O' level compared to every 152 candidates offering French, and only one at 'A' level to every seventy-two offering French. The Committee suggested that figure be raised to the level of German and French ratio; to do so the number of Russian teachers would have to increase from 350 to 1,500.

The re-orientation of humanistic studies in English universities

All this has had its influence on humanistic studies in

CONCLUSION

British universities, where English students engaged in studying foreign languages in England were described in 1947 by an interdepartmental Committee of Enquiry on Oriental, East European and African Studies as tending to become 'like a man who is always taking his car to pieces and never goes for a drive' (Scarborough Report, 1947, p. 30). On the same page their informant described his own activities as leading him 'to sink into a philological trance'. Victor Frank suggests 'the frightening realization of the inevitable political involvement ...has driven many gifted scholars in the field of Russian and Slavonic studies into the ivory tower of philology' (Laquer, 1965, p. 55).

Stimulus may, however, come from other quarters, notably the liberal arts divisions of the very technological institutions which the Russian 'threat' has virtually called into existence in England; here the history of science and technology and its impact on society have been invoked to provide a normative cultural balance to the curriculum. And as university curricula become more science-based, there has been a tendency to venture (albeit tentatively) into such fields, if only to offset the complaints of arts teachers like John Wain and Professor J. H. Plumb.

The 'provincialism' of concentrating on the 'purely Western' aspects of culture so deplored by the Scarbrough Committee in 1947 was re-emphasized fourteen years later by the University Grants Committee which pointed out the change over that period was 'so much that universities need to recognize this in the balance of their studies' (Hayter, 1960, p. 41).

This re-orientation has been helped by another factor.

The challenge of motivation

Though Lord Keynes denied that Russian communism

had made 'any contribution to our economic problems of intellectual interest or scientific value' (Keynes, 1931, p. 306), he admitted that 'as a religion' its forces were 'perhaps considerable'. 'It would not be difficult', commented E. H. Carr, 'to show that Keynes's own cardinal ideas had been applied in the Soviet Union and accepted as the basis of Soviet planning before they were worked out in the form of economic theory by Lord Keynes' (Carr, 1946, p. 35). As Carr put it:

> The Soviet Union has been generally accepted as the creator of contemporary 'planning', not so much because it first started planning or even because it did it more thoroughly than anyone else, but because it has most successfully combined the national and social aspects of planning into a single policy (ibid., p. 27).

It was what Lady Wootton called the 'ill-considered inferences from Russian experience' that really confused people's minds on the impact of economic planning upon both culture and civil freedoms (Wootton, 1945, p. 38). For Soviet plans have been carried out with the traditional Russian violence and harshness that goes back to Tsarist times when troops drove students out of universities. The 'limits of safe inference' from Russian planning, as she saw them, were two. First, that it is possible to do things in more ways than one. Second, that it is possible to plan up to a level of efficiency without recourse to industrial conscription.

The inclusion of public education and socialized medicine in the Soviet plans is seen, even by emigrés from Russia, to be by far their most important action. Polled by researchers in the Harvard Project on the Soviet Social System these emigrés confessed that despite the political slant of the Soviet educational system, it was 'something to be kept'. And the Soviet educational system obtained this verdict as often as all other specifically cited institutions combined (Inkeles and Bauer, 1959. pp. 132, 230). Today 'the one specifically Communist investment policy which is a definite advantage', as P.J.D. Wiles remarks, is that *'they try to use all their educated people and to educate only for use'*. This has further eroded what he calls the 'antitechnical snobbery'. Indeed the high rate of Soviet investment in education in post-war years will, according to Professor Alec Nove, help it to keep up its present fast pace since 'Much greater attention is paid to science, indeed, to knowledge as such, not only by the authorities but also among the people, since the U.S.S.R. has largely escaped the large scale 'commercialization of the moron' with its encouragement of 'mental laziness and ignorance' (Nove, 1965, p. 315).

This gives the Russians what C. P. Snow calls 'a clear edge. This is where their educational policy has already paid big dividends. They have such men to spare if they are needed. We just haven't, and the Americans aren't much better off' (Snow, 1964, p. 47-48).

Belief in educability

'The absolute assurance in the educability of children [which] was apparent at every level', was noted by the General Secretary of the Guild of Backward Children on his return to England (Segal, 1966, p. 68). It is not that the Russians train many more technicians and engineers, nor that they have a unique system for teaching them both intra- and extramurally; but that their social and educational policies are integrated, and that leisure, in an ever shorter working day, has its civilized outlets. During their leisure they may be assailed by propaganda but, as Isaac Deutscher said, 'it has at least the redeeming feature that it does not lower in the working man the level of his human interests' (Deutscher, 1960, p. 79). Speaking to a Canadian audience, Deutscher added, 'Despite all their faults the Russian "mass media" tend to instruct minds rather than stilt them; they try at least to develop in people a sense of community and solidarity; and sometimes they do it on a level of seriousness which should be the envy of the West'. The deeper springs of Russian motivation are a belief in tomorrow, that a shorter working day and ever more widely diffused educational facilities will be universal. 'This', said Deutscher, 'is an inspiring vista, and no poohpoohing will diminish its attraction. Has the West something better, non-realistic, or more inspiring to offer?' (ibid., p. 81).

In this faith, rather than in their recent achievement, lies the main influence of Soviet education today. It is the faith that one day the dream of the educational pioneers like Robert Owen and Marx in Britain, St Simon and Fourier in France and Chernyshevsky and Pisarev in Russia will materialize, that intellectual (*umstvennyi*) and physical (*fizicheskii*) labour will be component parts of the rounded personality. But they stress this will need a high level of technical progress, an abundance of material and cultural resources and the attainment of public self-government rather than state administration. As they see it, the key to this Valhalla is automation. This however does not mean that 'the worker in a future communist society will be able to specialize simultaneously in chemical production, in nuclear physics, electronics, engineering and so on' but that he will be equipped with 'a great technical and general knowledge, which enables him, when necessary, to change his job with minimum difficulty...and able to join in artistic activities and take part in social affairs' (Osipov, 1966, p. 185). These 'social affairs'

CONCLUSION

include national defence. Military training is now a subject in the senior classes of secondary schools (9th and 10th grades), in evening and in correspondence schools. Apart from its component of 'ideological preparation', this training includes the technological skills of modern defence (telephony, radar, car and motorcycle maintenance) as well as the attainment of physical fitness, military games and exercises. It is to be evaluated and recorded on the student's leaving certificate. Every school has its own 'military leader' who will be appointed by the local education authorities and military commissariats (T.E.S., 13 September, p. 443).

The grimness of Russian faith is unquestionable, and should be seen in the light of prophecies by the high priesthood of technocracy—the physicists. One of them, Academician Artsimovich, holds that 'in a few decades there will be more mathematicians and physicists in the U.S.S.R. than machine-tool operators and engine drivers'. Another, Peter Kapitza, a former member of the Cavendish Laboratory at Cambridge, suggests that half mankind will be engaged in scientific work and the other half supervise the automated factories (Davies, 1967, p. 18). At another level, one can see it in Soviet Science Fiction (Magidoff, 1963).

This 'drive to improve the rate of technological innovation', together with the much publicized 'science city', in turn focussed English attention on what Lord Snow called 'the harsh, objective and essential test of education: how many creative mathematicians did it produce who, by world standards could hold their own' (*The Times*, 8 March 1969). Citing Kolmogorov's 'school' of young mathematicians at Moscow as being able to 'take on the rest of the world' he posed a disturbing question to British egalitarians. An answer is still being sought.

Bibliography

ADLER, FRIEDRICH (1925), *The Anglo-Russian Report: A Criticism of the Report of the British Trades Union Delegation to Russia*, London: P. S. King.
ALBION, R. G. (1926), *Forests and Sea Power*, Cambridge, Massachussetts: Harvard University Press.
ALLEN, MEA (1964), *The Tradescants, Their Plants, Gardens and Museums 1570–1662*, London.
ANDERSON, M. S. (1954–5), 'English Views of Russia in the Seventeenth Century', *Slavonic and East European Review*, XXXIII, pp. 140–60.
ARMYTAGE, W. H. G. (1961), *Heavens Below*, Routledge & Kegan Paul.
ARNOLD, MATTHEW (1888), *Essays in Criticism*, Macmillan.
ASHBY, ERIC (1947), *Scientist in Russia*, Penguin.
ASHBY, ERIC (18 April 1954), 'Soviet Science is a Challenge to Us', *New York Times Magazine*.
BAGRIT, SIR LEON (1965), *The Age of Automation: The B.B.C. Reith Lectures*, Weidenfeld & Nicolson.
BARNES, LEONARD (1944), *Soviet Light on the Colonies*, Penguin.
BAUER, RAYMOND (1952), *The New Man in Soviet Psychology*, Cambridge, Massachussetts: Harvard University Press.
BENTHAM, JEREMY (1952), *Jeremy Bentham's Economic Writings*, edited by W. Stark, Allen & Unwin for the Royal Economic Society.
BERDYAEV, N. (1950), *Dream and Reality*, translated by Katherine Lampert, Geoffrey Bles.
BERNAL, J. D. (1939), *The Social Function of Science*, Routledge.

BIBLIOGRAPHY

BEVERIDGE, ALBERT J. (1903), *The Russian Advance*, Harper.
BIRKBECK, ROSE (1922), *Life and Letters of W. J. Birbeck*, Longmans Green.
BRAILSFORD, H. N. (1921), *The Russian Worker's Republic*, Allen & Unwin.
BRIGHT, JOHN and RODGERS, J. E. T. (1903), *Speeches on Questions of Public Policy by Richard Cobden, M.P.*, Macmillan.
BROWN, JOHN (1765), *Sermon on the Female Character and Education*, London: L. Davis & C. Reymers.
BROWN, JOHN (1765), *Thoughts on Civil Liberty on Licentiousness and Faction*, Newcastle-upon-Tyne.
BURNHAM, DAVID (1962), *The Managerial Revolution*, Penguin.
CARR, E. H. (1933), *The Romantic Exiles*, Gollancz.
CARR, E. H. (1946), *The Soviet Impact on the Western World*, Macmillan.
CARR, E. H. (1952), 'Some Unpublished Letters of Alexander Herzen', *Oxford Slavonic Papers*, III, pp. 80–124.
CHESTER, LEWIS; FAY, STEPHEN and YOUNG, HUGO (1967), *The Zinoviev Letters*, Heinemann.
CLARK, COLIN (1939), *A Critique of Russian Statistics*, Macmillan.
COATES, W. P. and ZELDA, K. (1934), *The Second Five-Year Plan of Development of the U.S.S.R.*, Methuen.
COUERDEROY, ERNEST (1854), *Hurrah!! ou la Revolution par les Cosaques*, London.
COLE, MARGARET I. (1945), *Beatrice Webb*, Longmans.
Communist Party of Great Britain (1943), *Britain's Schools*.
CREMIN, LAWRENCE A. (1961), *The Transformation of the School: Progressivism in American Education 1876–1957*, New York: A. A. Knopf.
CROSSMAN, RICHARD (1950), *The God that Failed*, Hamish Hamilton.
CROWTHER, J. G. (1932), *Industry and Education in Soviet Russia*, Heinemann.
DARLINGTON, T. (1909), 'Education in Russia', *Special Reports on Educational Subjects*, H.M.S.O., XXIII, cd. 4812.
DAVIES, JOHN (21 June 1968), 'Teamwork with Britain. The Soviet Union: A Special Report', *The Times*.
DAVIES, R. W. (1967), *Science and the Soviet Economy*, Birmingham: Publications Office of the University.
DAVIES, R, W. and BERRY, M. J. (1968), 'The Russian Scene', *Science and Technology in Europe*, edited by Eric Moonman, Penguin.

BIBLIOGRAPHY

DEUTSCHER, ISAAC (1960), *The Great Contest: Russia and the West*, Oxford University Press.

DOBB, MAURICE (1932), *Soviet Russia and the World*, London: Sidgwick & Jackson.

EISENHOWER, DWIGHT D. (1966), *The White House Years: Waging Peace, 1956–1961*, Heinemann.

ELLIS, HAVELOCK (1890), *The New Spirit*, London: Bell.

FISHER, R. T. (1959), *Pattern for Soviet Youth: A Study of the Congress of the Komosol, 1918–1954*, Oxford University Press.

FLETCHER, GILES (1966), *Of the Russe Commonwealth: Facsimile Edition with Variants*, Cambridge, Massachusetts: Harvard University Press.

Foreign Office (1947), *Report of the Interdepartmental Commission of Enquiry on Oriental East European and African Studies* (the Scarborough Report), H.M.S.O.

FRIEDMAN, ARTHUR (1966), *Collected Works of Oliver Goldsmith*, Oxford: Clarendon Press.

GALBRAITH, J. K. (1958), *The Affluent Society*, Hamish Hamilton.

GARNETT, CONSTANCE (translator) (1926), *Fathers and Children* by Ivan Turgenev, Heinemann.

GERSCHENKRON, ALEXANDER (1947), 'The Rate of Industrial Growth in Russia Since 1885', *Journal of Economic History*, VII, Supplement 7, pp. 144–74.

GLEASON, JOHN H. (1950), *The Genesis of Russophobia in Great Britain*, Cambridge, Massachusetts: Harvard University Press.

GOODE, W. T. (1920), *Bolshevism at Work*, Allen & Unwin.

GOODE, W. T. (editor) (1929), *Schools in the New Russia*, London: Williams & Norgate.

GOODMAN, ANN S. and FESHBACH (1967). *Estimates and Projections of Educational Attainment in the U.S.S.R., 1950–1985*, Washington, Government Printing Office, U.S. Bureau of the International Population Reports Series, No. 16, p. 91.

GOSSE, EDMUND (editor) (1890), *Work While Ye Have the Light*, by Leo Tolstoy, Heinemann.

GROVES, REGINALD (1967), *Conrad Noel and the Thaxted Movement*, London: Merlin Press.

HADEN GUEST, L. (1920), 'Visits to Educational Institutions', *Report of the British Labour Delegation to Russia, 1920*, T.U.C. and the Labour Party.

BIBLIOGRAPHY

HAKLUYT, RICHARD (1903), *The Principal Navigations of the English Nation*, Glasgow: James Maclehose.

Hakluyt Society (1856), *A Relacion or Memorial abstracted out of Sir Jerome Horsey his Trauelles*, London.

HANS, N. (1961–2), 'Dumaresq, Brown and Some Early Educational Projects of Catherine II', *Slavonic and East European Review*, XL, pp. 229–235.

HANSARD (H. of C.), 137 (16 March 1855) 640–672; 420 (22 March 1946) 2184–2250; 441 (31 July 1947) 647–743; 540 (26 April 1955) 768–890; 554 (21 June 1956) 1639–1762; 567 (22 March 1957) 661–761 : (H. of L.), 200 (21 November 1956) 426–525; 223 (11 May 1960) 615–623.

HAYTER, SIR WILLIAM (1960), *Diplomacy of the Great Powers*, Hamilton.

HEILBRUN, CAROLYN G. (1961), *The Garnett Family*, Allen & Unwin.

H.M.S.O. (1930), *Certain Legislation Reflecting Religion in Force in the Union of Socialist Soviet Republics*, Cmd. 3641.

H.M.S.O. (1926), *Communist Papers: Documents Selected from Those Obtained on the Arrest of the Communist Leaders on the 14th and 21st October 1925*, Cmd. 2682.

H.M.S.O. (1927), *Documents Illustrating the Hostile Activities of the Soviet Government and Third International against Great Britain*, Cmd. 2874.

H.M.S.O. (1909), *Education in Russia: Board of Education Special Reports*.

H.M.S.O. (1963), *Higher Education: the Robbins Report*.

H.M.S.O. (1966), *Report of the Select Committee on Education*, Parliamentary Papers, XVI.

H.M.S.O. (1966), *Technical Education*, Cmd. 9703.

HINDUS, MAURICE (1942), *Mother Russia*, London: Readers Union.

HUGHES, E. (1949), 'Sir Charles Trevelyan and Civil Service Reform 1853–5', *English Historical Review*, LXIV, pp. 53–88, 206–234.

HUTCHINS, JOHN H. (1940), *Jonas Hanway 1712–1786*, London: Society for the Promotion of Christian Knowledge.

HUTTON, R. S. (1943), *Higher Technical Education*, City and Guilds of London Institute.

Impact of the Russian Revolution 1917–1967, with an introductory essay by Arnold Toynbee (1967), Oxford University Press for the Royal Institute of International Affairs.

BIBLIOGRAPHY

JOHNSON, WILLIAM E. H. (1950), *Russia's Educational Heritage*, New Jersey, New Brunswick; Rutgers University Press.

JOLLIFFE, JOHN (Autumn 1967), 'Lord Carlisle's Embassy to Moscow', *Cornhill Magazine*, No. 1053, pp. 217–237.

JORAVSKY, DAVID (1961), 'The History of Technology in Soviet Russia and Marxist Doctrine', *Technology and Culture*, II, pp. 5–10.

KELLER, WERNER (1961), *Are the Russians Ten Feet Tall?*, translated by Constantine Fitzgibbon, Thames & Hudson.

KEMP, BETTY (1959–60), 'Sir Francis Dashwood's Diary of His Visit to St Petersburg in 1933', *Slavonic and East European Review*, XXXVII, pp. 194–222.

KEYNES, JOHN MAYNARD (1931), *Essays in Persuasion*, Macmillan.

KNIGHT, ARTHUR (1959), *The Liveliest Art: A Panoramic History of the Movies*, New York: Mentor Books.

KROPOTKIN, P. (October 1893), 'On the Teaching of Physiography', *Geographical Journal*. (The editor misspelt his name as Krapotkin.)

LAQUEUR, WALTER (1965), *Russia and Germany, a Century of Conflict*, Weidenfeld & Nicolson.

LASKI, HAROLD J. (1948), *Communist Manifesto. Socialist Landmark*, Allen & Unwin.

LEEMING, H. (1968), 'Russian Works in Sixteenth-Century English Sources', *Slavonic and East European Review*, XLVI, pp. 1–30, (1969) XLVII, pp. 11–36.

LEHRMAN, EDGAR H. (1961), *Turgenev's Letters: A Selection*, New York: A. A. Knopf.

LILGE, FREDERIC (1958), *Anton Semyonovich Makarenko; An Analysis of His Educational Ideas in the Context of Soviet Society*, Berkeley and Los Angeles: University of California, Publications in Education Vol. 13, No. 1, pp. 1–52.

LONG, J. (1874), *The Present Position of Russia in Central Asia in Relation to the Spread of Christianity and Civilization in the East*, London: Gilbert & Rivington.

LOUGH, A. G. (1962), *The Influence of John Mason Neale*, London: Society for the Promotion of Christian Knowledge.

LOWRIE, D. A. (1960), *Rebellious Prophet: a Life of Nicolai Berdyaev*, Gollancz.

MCKENZIE, KERMIT E. (1964), *Comintern and World Revolution 1928–1943*, London: Columbia University Press.

MACK, MARY P. (1962), *Jeremy Bentham, an Odyssey of Ideas 1748–1792*, Heinemann.

BIBLIOGRAPHY

MACKINDER, H. J. (1904, reprinted 1943), 'The Geographical Pivot of History', *Geographical Journal*, XXIII, pp. 421–37.

MACKINDER, H. J. (July 1943), 'The Round World and the Winning of the Peace', *Foreign Affairs*.

MAGIDOFF, ROBERT (1963), *Russian Science Fiction: an Anthology*, Allen & Unwin.

MAINWARING, MARION (1952), 'Arnold and Tolstoy', *Nineteenth-Century Fiction*, Berkeley.

MAKARENKO, A. (1936), *The Road to Life*, translated by S. Garry, London: Stanley Nott.

MANDEL, WILLIAM M. (1968), 'Arthur Ransome: Eyewitness in Russia 1919', *Slavonic and East European Review*, pp. 290–295.

MARINE SOCIETY (1952), *A Short History of the Marine Society Together with the Act of Incorporation and the Bye-Laws*, 11th edn., Salisbury: Salisbury Press.

MARX, KARL (1939), *Capital*, Dent, Everyman edn.

MARX, K., ENGELS, F. and LENIN, V. I. (1967), *On Scientific Communism*, Moscow: Progress Publishers.

MAUDE, AYLMER (1911), *The Life of Tolstoy: Later Years*, Constable.

MAYHEW, HENRY (1864), *German Life and Manners as seen in Saxony at the Present Day*, W. H. Allen.

MEDYNSKY, EUGENE (1943), 'Anton Makarenko–Soviet Educator', *V.O.K.S. Bulletin*, Nos. 9 & 10, and 31–35.

MICHELL, T. (1866), 'The Present State of Trade Between Great Britain and Russia', H.M.S.O., Reports of Secretaries of Embassy and Legation, Vol. 72.

MILTON, JOHN (1682), *A Brief History of Muscovia, and of other less-known Countries lying Eastern of Russia as far as Cathay: Gathered from the Writings of Several Eye-Witnesses*, London.

MITCHISON, G. R. (1934), *The First Worker's Government or New Times for Henry Dubb*, Gollancz.

MONTGOMERY, R. J. (1965), *Examinations: An Account of their Evolution as Administrative Devices*, Longmans.

MORREN, D. G. (1967), 'Donald Mackenzie Wallace and British Russophilism, 1870–1919', *Canadian Slavonic Papers*, IX, No. 2, pp. 145–295, Toronto: University of Toronto Press.

MORRISON, HERBERT et al. (1944), *Can Planning be Democratic? A Collection of Essays Prepared for the Fabian Society*, Routledge.

BIBLIOGRAPHY

NEEDHAM, JOSEPH (1946), *History is on Our Side*, Allen & Unwin.
NOVE, ALEC (1965), *The Soviet Economy*, Allen & Unwin.
ORWELL, GEORGE (1961), *Collected Essays*, London: Mercury Books.
OSIPOV, GEORGE (editor) (1966), *Industry and Labour in the U.S.S.R.*, Tavistock.
PARTRIDGE, MONICA (1962-3), 'Slavonic Themes in English Poetry of the Nineteenth Century', *Slavonic and East European Review*, XLI, pp. 420–441.
PAVLOV, I. P. (1902), *The Work of the Digestive Glands*, translated by W. H. Thompson, London: Charles Griffin.
PUDOVKIN, V. I. (1933), *Film Technique*, translated and annotated by Ivor Montague, Newnes.
PUTNAM, PETER (editor) (1952), *Seven Britons in Imperial Russia, 1698-1812*, Princeton University Press.
RANSOME, ARTHUR (1919), *Six Weeks in Russia*, Allen & Unwin.
READING, D. K. (1938), *The Anglo-Russian Commercial Treaty of 1734*, New Haven: Yale Historical Publications, Miscellany Vol. 321.
REDFERN, PERCY (1946), *Journey to Understanding*, Allen & Unwin.
REDL, HELENE B. (1964), *Soviet Educators on Education*, Collier-Macmillan.
RIDLEY, J. CARTMEL (1898), *Reminiscences of Russia, the Ural Mountains and Adjoining Siberian District in 1879*, Newcastle-upon-Tyne: Andrew Reid.
RUSSELL, BERTRAND (1932), *Education and the Social Order*, Allen & Unwin.
Russia, *The Official Report of the British Trades Union Delegation to Russia and Caucasia, November and December 1924*, London: T.U.C.
SAMPSON, ANTHONY (1967), *Macmillan: A Study in Ambiguity*, Allen Lane, The Penguin Press.
SAMUELS, STUART (1966), 'The Left Book Club', *Journal of Contemporary History*, I, No. 2, pp. 65–86.
Scarborough Report, see Foreign Office.
SCHUYLER, EUGENE (1928), 'A Secret Press in England', *The Bookman's Journal*, XV, p. 217; XVI, p. 278.
SEGAL, S. S. (1966), *Backward Children in the U.S.S.R.*, Leeds: E. J. Arnold.
SEELEY, J. R. (1884), *The Expansion of England*, Macmillan.

BIBLIOGRAPHY

SHARP, JAMES A. (1845), *On the Establishment of Navigation Institutions at the Outports*, R. B. Bate.

SHARP, JAMES A. (1858), *Memoirs of the Life and Services of Rear-Admiral Sir William Symonds*, Longman Brown Green, Longmans & Roberts.

SIMMONS, E. J. (1935), *English Literature and Culture in Russia 1553–1840*, Cambridge, Massachusetts: Harvard University Press.

SIMMONS, J. S. G. (1950), 'H. W. Ludolph and the Printing of his *Grammatica Russica* at Oxford in 1696', *Oxford Slavonic Papers*, I, pp. 104–129.

SIMMONS, J. S. G. (1952), 'Slavonic Studies at Oxford: the Proposed Slavonic Chair at the Taylor Institution in 1844', *Oxford Slavonic Papers*, III, pp. 125–151.

SIMON, E. D. (editor) (1937), *Moscow in the Making*, Longmans.

SNOW, C. P. (1964). *The Two Cultures: and a Second Look*, Cambridge University Press.

SNOWDEN, MRS PHILIP (1920), *Through Bolshevik Russia*, Cassell.

Soviet Science and Technology (1962), *A Bibliograhpy of the State of the Art 1959–61*, Washington: Library of Congress.

STANLEY, A. P. (1890), *The Life and Correspondence of Thomas Arnold D.D.*, Ward Lock.

STARK, W. (editor) (1952), *Jeremy Bentham's Economic Writings*, Allen & Unwin for Royal Economic Society.

STEAD, W. T. (1888), *The Truth About Russia*, Cassell.

STEPNIAK, S. (1895), *Nihilism As It Is*, T. Fisher Unwin.

STRUMILIN, S. G. (1964), *Man, Society and the Future*, New York: Cross Currents.

The Times, Russian Supplements, 15 January 1911; 18 January 1960; 6 November 1967; 8 March 1969.

The Times Educational Supplement: 29 December 1945; 4 May 1946; 29 November 1947; 25 September 1948; 14 October 1949; 14 September 1951; 19 October 1951; 14 November 1952; 3 September 1954; 29 April 1955; 30 December 1955; 24 February 1956; 9, 11 & 17 October 1957; 13 September 1968.

THOMPSON, KENNETH W. (1955), 'Toynbee's Approach to History Reviewed', *Ethics*, LXV, pp. 287–303.

TOLSTOY, LEO (1937), *Works*, translated by Aylmer Maude, London: Humphrey Milford.

TOYNBEE, ARNOLD (1939–61), *A Study of History* (in 12 vols.), Oxford University Press.

BIBLIOGRAPHY

TRILLING, LIONEL (1955), *Soviet Education in Aeronautics: A Case Study*, Massachusetts Institute of Technology.

TURNER, N. D. S., WARREN, F. G. E. and NOLAN, J. P. (1867), *Tour of Artillery Officers in Russia*, Eyre & Spottiswoode for H.M.S.O.

UNWIN, SIR STANLEY (1960), *The Truth About a Publisher, an Autobiographical Record*, Allen & Unwin.

URNESS, CAROL (1967), *A Naturalist in Russia: Letters from Peter Simon Pallas to Thomas Pennant*, Minneapolis: University of Minnesota Press.

VASLEF, NICHOLAS P., 'Bulgarin and the Development of the Russian Utopian Genre', *The Slavic and East European Journal*, XII, No. 1, pp. 35–43.

WALLACE, DONALD MACKENZIE (1877), *Russia*, Cassell.

WALLACE, DONALD MACKENZIE (1876), 'The Territorial Expansion of Russia', *Fortnightly Review*, XX, pp. 145–166.

WALSH, WALTER (1921), *The Republic of God*, Daniel.

WEBB, SIDNEY and BEATRICE (1935), *Soviet Communism: A New Civilization?*, London: privately printed.

WEST, CHARLES C. (1958), *Communism and the Theologians*, London: S.C.M. Press.

WILLAN, T. S. (1956), *The Early History of the Russian Company 1553–1603*, Manchester: The University Press.

WILLIAMS, BERYL J. (1966), 'The Strategic Background to the Anglo-Russian Entente of August 1907', *Historical Journal*, IX, pp. 360–73.

WOODCOCK, G. and AVAKUMOVIC, I. (1950), *The Anarchist Prince: A Biographical Study of Peter Kropotkin*, London: T. V. Broadman.

WOOLF, VIRGINIA (1932), 'The Russian Point of View', *The Common Reader*, 1st series, Hogarth Press.

WOOTTON, BARBARA (1945), *Freedom Under Planning*, Allen & Unwin.

WOOTTON, BARBARA (1934), *Plan or No Plan*, Gollancz.

ZERNOV, NICHOLAS (1944), *The Russians and Their Church*, London: Society for the Promotion of Christian Knowledge.

ZVORIKINE, A. (1961), 'The History of Technology as a Science and as a Branch of Learning: A Soviet View', *Technology and Culture*, II, pp. 1–4.